Soccer Goalkeeper Training

For Beth and Lisa

Tony Englund I John Pascarella

SOCCER
GOALKEEPER
TRAINING
The Comprehensive Guide

Meyer & Meyer Sport

SOCCER
GOALKEEPER
TRAINING

British Library Cataloguing in Publication Data
A catalogue record for this book is available from the British Library

Soccer Goalkeeper Training
Maidenhead: Meyer & Meyer Sport (UK) Ltd., 2017
ISBN: 978-1-78255-107-2

© 2017 by Meyer & Meyer Sport (UK) Ltd.
Aachen, Auckland, Beirut, Cairo, Cape Town, Dubai, Hägendorf, Hong Kong,
Indianapolis, Manila, New Delhi, Singapore, Sydney, Tehran, Vienna
Member of the World Sport Publishers' Association (WSPA)
Manufacturing: Print Consult, Munich
ISBN: 978-1-78255-107-2
Email: info@m-m-sports.com
www.m-m-sports.com

CONTENTS

ACKNOWLEDGMENTS

TONY ENGLUND

In 2015, I enrolled in the National Soccer Coaches Association of America's Master Coach Certificate program. This was an outstanding program, featuring the opportunity to network with and learn from elite coaches from around the world. The greatest take-away for me, both professionally and personally, was the opportunity to meet and work with John Pascarella of Major League Soccer's Sporting Kansas City. Coach Pascarella is a coach's coach: bright, charismatic, visionary, thoughtful, inquisitive and dynamic. Through the NSCAA's program design and Coach Pascarella's remarkable generosity, I have had the opportunity to observe many first-team training sessions and matches, enjoyed tremendous access to the first-team and academy staff and, most critically, a chance to learn much more about the art and science of goalkeeper coaching through many lengthy conversations with John. He is a valued colleague, mentor and friend, and I will always be thankful to him for undertaking this project with me in spite of his busy schedule.

Jeff Cassar and Daryl Shore of Major League Soccer's Real Salt Lake graciously agreed to write the foreword to the book and I am thankful for their contributions. Mateus Manoel, the outstanding Head Fitness Coach at Sporting Kansas City, and Patrick Mannix of his staff, as well as Josh McAllister of Swope Park Rangers added to and reviewed the fitness-related information in the book, and their assistance is gratefully acknowledged.

Ian Barker at the NSCAA encouraged me to register for the Master Coach course, steered me away from several other project ideas and assigned John Pascarella as my course mentor, and I am very appreciative of his guidance in the course and his leadership of the NSCAA's coaching education in general.

Kristina Oltrogge at Meyer & Meyer has been a consummate professional in working with John and me throughout the writing process, and we appreciate her patience and diligence. Thanks to Manuel Morschel as well for his willingness to publish our work.

Nathan Klonecki and my colleagues at Sporting St. Croix Academy and Soccer Club in St. Paul have supported this project from its inception, and I am indebted to Nathan and the goalkeeper coaching staff for their feedback and the ideas that have been incorporated into the book.

Payton Spencer, Oscar Mulvaney, Lauren Thormodsgard and my stepdaughter Tess Wilder gave considerable time to appear in the photos for the book. They are outstanding people and goalkeepers, and I am thankful for their help.

Karen McCullough gave permission to use her photos in the book. Thank you, Karen.

Tony and Carole Englund, my parents, continue to be life's best coaches, and their influence is paramount in my coaching and life. Thank you both, as always.

My wife Beth has been a constant source of support and inspiration during the writing of the manuscript. From endless trips and hotel stays across the country with my teams to the late-night clattering of my keyboard, she has cheerfully adopted the soccer life. My love and thanks to her for making the journey so much more meaningful and enjoyable.

JOHN PASCARELLA

In finishing this book (and our season coming to a premature end), I'm finally able to give some prolonged thought to how much help I've had and sacrificed the most while I was writing this book were my wife Lisa and my four children, Kara, Cassie, John-Patrick and Jordan. During my time as a player, coach, presenter or author, Lisa always provides the support and guidance needed, especially when things aren't turning out the way I had hoped. She always gives me perspective and makes me a better version of myself than I could hope to be on my own. Each of my children have qualities that make me proud and during the writing of this book I've found myself wishing I had a little more of those qualities that they possess in spades.

Whenever I was fighting against time and feeling tired and sorry for myself, I'd think of Kara's work ethic. Although a senior in high school, she plays club soccer and has a minimum of two jobs at any one time, sometimes leaving at 5:00 in the morning to start her first one…on Saturday morning, no less. What high school kid does that?! She always likes to say that I love her the most out of all my children—any parent would tell you that you love them all equally and for different reasons—but I'd like to say here, for the record, that I've loved her the longest!

Cassie is our perfectionist. At times, when I was writing and frustrated with the process of trying to get my thoughts onto paper I would often do the bare minimum and think it was good enough. Eventually, my thoughts would turn to her and the way she is constantly revising and tweaking her projects and homework, striving to get it done perfectly, which would then cause me to come back to my writing and try to make it better and more worthwhile to the reader.

John-Patrick is my only son and plays for our U14 academy team at Sporting KC. Whenever I think I'm becoming a better coach I try explaining something related to the game to him and get the same look my dogs give me when they hear something strange and tilt their heads to the side. That's when I know I need to reconsider how to get my point across. On those occasions, he never ceases to amaze me by eventually grasping the concept and then repeating it back to me in much simpler terms and language. That quality has been especially helpful to me during this project.

Jordan, my youngest, is the most energetic and brutally honest kid you'll meet. That combination always keeps me in check when my motivation to write waivers or the quality of my writing is poor. She is also the one that enjoys hugging the most. Often, I'd sit at the table and start writing only to get up 15 minutes later frustrated that I couldn't get down on paper what was in my head. Jordy would ask, "Are you done already, Dad?" Invariably I'd say to her in various ways, I'm not enjoying this and really, not very good at it. She'd look at me in that cute and conniving little way that all youngest siblings do and say "Do you want to snuggle on the couch?" I didn't need another excuse to walk away from the writing. Eventually, while sitting with her, she would repeat to me something along the lines of "Dad, you always tell me when I get frustrated just to stick with it" or "Dad, you always say 'action comes before motivation,' so just start writing again and you'll get motivated as you go...right?" Suffice it to say, this book would never have been finished if it weren't for my wife and kids!

For the past eight seasons, I've been blessed to work for the most forward thinking (and one of the most successful) clubs in Major League Soccer. I want to thank our manager Peter Vermes for the opportunity to work with him and for the trust he has in me to allow me to coach in a way that I see fit, allowing me to become a better coach along the way. It takes a very secure head coach to allow you to work with true freedom, and he has given me all the freedom I could have asked for in implementing my ideas. Many of the training activities in this book have been tweaked and improved from my previous work because he has created the environment and allowed me the freedom to experiment and try to find the best formula for each of our goalkeepers.

I've also been spoiled to work with three tremendous conditioning coaches at Sporting Kansas City. Over the last few years I've relied on Mateus Manoel, Patrick Mannix and Josh McAllister to create functional training exercises and activities that mask the fitness component while bringing about the technical and tactical aspects we are trying to improve. Over time they've helped me become a better and more efficient coach as well as contributing greatly to the areas of physiology, warm-up, cool-down and nutrition in this book.

There are so many good people working and volunteering their time for the NSCAA. Their conventions, coaching courses and various forums have given me an outlet to share

much of the information I've gathered over the years with others seeking to exchange ideas on the game. These exchanges have provoked many thoughts on the game that I may not have realized without their help and input. Some of the ideas presented in this book have literally been stolen from some of these folks and adapted for my coaching purposes with the various goalkeepers I've had over the years. One of those people is Tony Dicicco. He has been a consistent influence in my life since college, when he hired me to work for his Soccer Plus Goalkeeper Camps around the country. Working with him helped me form my outlook and philosophy on coaching goalkeepers as I'm always try to catch them being good!

I would also like to thank both Jeff Cassar and Daryl Shore for contributing the foreword for this book as well as insights into our league and our profession since I was hired by Sporting Kansas City in 2009. Both have played in Major League Soccer as goalkeepers. Both were goalkeeping coaches in the league and Daryl currently continues in that role with Real Salt Lake. Both have also been head coaches, Jeff currently with RSL in Major League Soccer and Daryl with the Fort Lauderdale Strikers in the NASL. Daryl and I have known each other since college and hopefully the things he knows about me will go with him to his grave.

Finally, I'd like to thank Tony Englund. This book was his idea and he was truly the inspiration behind it. I've had a chance to work with him on two occasions and I'd do it again. Why? Because every time we have a discussion, regardless if it's about the game, raising kids or anything else, I learn something. You can't get enough of people like that in your life.

FOREWORD
BY DARYL SHORE

Alabama, 1988. I was an incoming freshman set to attend Birmingham–Southern College (BSC) on a soccer scholarship. During the summers, our coach held soccer camp, and this year, for the second year in a row, our coach had secured Tony Schumacher (my idol growing up) to headline the "Excellence Through Fundamentals" soccer camp. I had hoped to be able to attend the camp and learn from one of the world's greatest, but since I was enrolled in summer classes, I was not allowed to participate. So in the evenings, I'd watch the camp action from afar. One night when I was sitting in the stands, I saw a young goalkeeper working the camp, "hamming" it up with Schumacher and the others. I watched this guy closely because his goalkeeping techniques were similar to mine— particularly his quickness, reactions, and smart attitude. Intrigued by his qualities, it was then I decided that I was going to get to know this guy.

This was my first introduction to John Pascarella, professional goalkeeper from Penn State University, now plying his trade in Peru. I didn't really get to know John that well until the following year when he returned to BSC to work the camp. I was now on my college team as an up-and-coming goalkeeper with dreams of playing professionally. John's contract stated that he could return to BSC to work the camp for a week, especially since Tony Schumacher was scheduled to return. Unbeknownst to us, Schumacher didn't show up. As our coach tried to figure out how to handle the situation, John took control and said, "Don't worry, boys, we'll run the goalkeeper part of this camp, and no one will miss Tony." I spent that entire week coaching with John, training with him in our off time, and picking his brain at night. John was a confident guy, but one thing was for sure, he told it like it was and didn't hide from the truth. He was honest and worked his butt off when he trained and coached the campers, but most importantly, he was always in good spirits and made sure that he and everyone around him were enjoying themselves both on and off the soccer field. It was then that I knew John was going to have a long career in coaching after his playing career as a professional goalkeeper.

Florida, 2009. Time passed, and we went our separate ways. As I continued to chase the dream of becoming a professional player, John finished up his playing career in 1997 and climbed the ranks of becoming one of the best goalkeeper coaches in in the US. John put his time in coaching the US Soccer semi-pro and pro circuits as well as the college game. With his background, not only in goalkeeping but in exercise science, it was only a matter of time until he would get his chance to work in America's top league, Major League Soccer. When John joined the Sporting Kansas City staff in 2009, as both the goalkeeper coach and the strength and conditioning coach, I was on the staff with the Chicago Fire. Though we had not talked for quite some years, we reconnected during preseason in Bradenton, Florida, and it was there I remembered what I thought back in 1989: This guy was good at what he did. It takes loyalty and perseverance to stay on a coaching staff for eight years, and those are two of John's strongest attributes.

While I was an assistant coach with the Fire, I was also the director of Soccer Operations for a soccer combine company called InfoSport. Upon reconnecting that preseason, I asked John if he would be interested in joining our staff, and he immediately agreed and has been a mainstay on the InfoSport coaching staff since 2010. He was instrumental in assisting us, adding a goalkeepers-only portion to the combine—another example of how John takes leadership responsibility and runs with it. Once again, he reminded me of why he has been and still is a very successful goalkeeper coach. John's ability to work with goalkeepers of all ages meant it was just a matter of time before he would coach an MLS Goalkeeper of the Year (Jimmy Nielson, 2013).

2016. John Pascarella has coached goalkeepers at all levels. He has now partnered with NSCAA Master Coach and author, Tony Englund, and together they have written *Soccer Goalkeeper Coaching: The Comprehensive Guide* for past, current, and aspiring goalkeepers to read. John and Tony set out to address the need to provide an accessible, thorough book on goalkeeper coaching that would appeal to specialists, team coaches, and parents, and they've done a marvelous job. It is clear that they have thought through every aspect of goalkeeper coaching and drawn together the very best material to write this volume. The book has hundreds of exercises and tips, as well as many thoughtful analyses of the goalkeeping position. *Soccer Goalkeeper Training: The Comprehensive Guide* is an important asset to our staff and those interested in improving their goalkeepers at every level.

I am honored to call John Pascarella not only a colleague in the sport, but more importantly, a friend. He and Tony have raised the bar in goalkeeper coaching with this new and important book.

Mark up and don't lose your man!

Daryl Shore, Director of Goalkeeping, Real Salt Lake (MLS)

INTRODUCTION

OVERVIEW: FOR SPECIALISTS, TEAM COACHES AND PARENTS

Frequently, goalkeepers are classified by coaches and teammates as a breed apart. Many think one would have to be crazy to volunteer to play goalkeeper in soccer. However, virtually everyone involved in the game would concede that without an accomplished goalkeeper, a team's potential is extremely limited. Indeed, the current men's World Cup champions Germany are led by their goalkeeper, Manuel Neuer, arguably the best at his position in the world at the time of this writing.

Goalkeeping is a very specialized position and there have been increasingly impressive efforts in recent years to assemble thorough coaching and training plans for goalkeepers of every level. Indeed, Tim Mulqueen's *The Complete Soccer Goalkeeper* (Human Kinetics, 2010) is the most recent and well-written example. The current effort, the authors hope, will be the most thorough and accessible effort to date. This book, it should be noted, is written with the goalkeeper specialist, team coach and parent in mind. Whether one trains goalkeepers every week or has a child interested in trying the position, this volume is designed to be easy to follow and packed with information and training ideas. Specialists and team coaches will find thorough explanations of tactical concepts and a wide variety of training ideas to enrich their planning. Parents will find the technical descriptions, many photos and diagrams helpful for working with their children as they learn to play goalkeeper.

Topics covered include all standard technical movements, saves and distribution, tactical concepts from dealing with through-balls to defending set-pieces, a chapter on the psychological challenges of playing and coaching the position, fitness, and more. Finally, the last chapter of the book includes dozens of exercises organized by topic and designed to provide interesting, varied and challenging training to goalkeepers at every level.

WHO CAN BE A GOALKEEPER? THE PROFILE

Not everyone can play as a goalkeeper. It takes a different temperament to play the position than that of an outfield player, which is probably why many people say that goalkeepers are crazy. However, nothing could be further from the truth. It takes such a varied set of physical and psychological skills as well as a deep understanding of the game to achieve success in the goalkeeper position that the reality is many goalkeepers are the most cerebral player on the team.

THE FOUR PILLARS OF THE GAME

As an approach to the question "Who can be a goalkeeper?" it is useful to break down the four pillars of the game and show how they relate to the goalkeeping position and ask questions that parents, players and coaches should ask to determine if the position is right for them. Obviously, the weighting of many of these characteristics changes based on the age and level of the player. For example, height isn't necessarily important to a 13-year-old goalkeeper but his size will become increasingly important as he gets older and enters the collegiate or professional game.

1. *Technical profile: Can the goalkeeper keep the ball out of the goal and can we play through him?*

At the end of the day the goalkeeper is most strongly evaluated on his ability to keep the opposition from scoring goals. Can he handle shots cleanly regardless of catching or deflecting them? Does he have good rhythm and timing in crossing situations so he can confidently catch and punch crosses? Is he able to spread at an attacker's feet in 1-vs.-1 situations?

In addition to dealing with shots and crosses, goalkeepers who are competent with their feet can also help their defenders play out of tough situations if they are good enough to deal securely with back-passes and participate in build-up play instead of just kicking the ball long, down the field.

These are some of the questions and areas that need to be evaluated when looking at whether a player can handle the technical aspects of the position.

2. *Tactical profile: Can he read the game and make good decisions?*

The fact that the goalkeeper plays behind everyone and has a view of the entire field is a great advantage to those that understand what's unfolding in front of them. Does he understand the game well enough to direct players in front of him with clear, concise and accurate information? Can he make correct decisions under extreme pressure, and can he read the game quickly and accurately enough to put his own players in positions to shut down the opposition's opportunities before they become dangerous chances?

This requires that the goalkeeper understand the game and will find it to his advantage to spend time as a youth player in positions other than goalkeeper so as to gain an understanding of the mentality and strategy of attacking players. This insight is an advantage to those who put the time in to learn the game as a whole, not just from the perspective of a goalkeeper.

To summarize, if a goalkeeper can be the eyes and conscience of the team as things are happening in front of him he can diffuse many difficult situations before they occur.

3. *Psychological profile: Does he have a presence?*

If a goalkeeper can instill a sense of confidence in his teammates he is worth his weight in gold.

Does he have a strong and positive body language? Is he mentally strong? Is he brave enough to put himself into situations where there will likely be contact to make a save? Does he have the leadership qualities to direct the players in front of him and take command of situations through action and communication? Can he recover from an error to make a crucial save when the game is on the line? These are questions that players need to be able to answer with a resounding "Yes!" if they are to play with courage and conviction going forward in attack.

These intangibles are what often set the best apart from the rest.

4. *Physical profile: Does he look the part?*

The physical presence of the goalkeeper becomes a critical element at the advanced levels of the game. Taller, stronger goalkeepers find it easier to control their area, defending crosses and heavy-paced shots. The demands of the position require that the goalkeeper have the ability to move powerfully, especially over short distances and in their jumping and diving actions. Good balance, coordination and agility are also a requirement because of how many times he needs to change speed and direction as he is following the action. His ability to contort his body in space (kinesthetic sense) can also be a major help to the goalkeeper, especially if he is already in motion to make a save and the ball is deflected and changes direction.

So, Who Can Be a Goalkeeper?

At the younger ages, virtually any child can try goalkeeping, and indeed, this is a fundamental means of learning about the game for all players. Serving as a goalkeeper adds appreciation for the challenges of the position, as well as a radically expanded skill set. As children advance within the game, the elements emphasized here become a more stringent formula for measuring the potential of a goalkeeper. As mentioned

earlier, the qualities listed in these profiles are all important but what is most crucial is the combination and complementary nature of the qualities. For example, the goalkeeper may lack some top-quality athleticism but may be able to make up for it with a superior ability to understand, read and anticipate action in the game. The composite makeup of the goalkeeper and how he fits into the team's overall playing style is the overriding factor.

AGE-APPROPRIATE TRAINING FOR GOALKEEPERS: AGE GROUP EMPHASIS AND TRAINING PRIORITIES

Before the age of twelve there should be very little focus on specialization training as a goalkeeper. At younger ages it is more important for the players to play and train in a variety of positions and even a variety of sports. Why? The reason for playing multiple positions is to develop an understanding of the game as a whole and not just how to defend the goal. Playing and training as a field player will engender in a goalkeeper a different and more varied perspective of the game than if he simply plays as a goalkeeper from day one.

The photos below share ideas for some possession games or games to goal that can be varied to include goalkeepers playing either centrally or as bumpers. When the coach includes restrictions such as passes into feet needing to be played with feet and balls passed in the air needing to be caught, he can now arrange activities and games that incorporate goalkeepers into the session to play and understand the bigger picture of the entire game while incorporating the goalkeepers into team training.

4-vs.-4 plus three with goalkeepers.

2-vs.-2 plus three with goalkeepers (neutral players on one touch).

19

The rationale for playing multiple sports is the greater the general pool of motor skills developed at a young age, the more potential for elite athletic movement and coordination at an older level. Stated another way, the broader the base of movement skill, the better the potential for athletic excellence down the road.

Based on this philosophy, the focus throughout this book is on coordination, movement, kinetics and overall athleticism as a broad base for the more specific skills of soccer and, even more specifically, the skills of a goalkeeper in soccer. Exercises such as the ones below should constitute the basis of the physical and technical drills that young goalkeepers should participate in during training to ensure a good foundation of movement skills and athleticism as they progress to the more advanced levels.

Examples of exercises designed to improve young goalkeepers' kinesthetic sense, coordination and agility.

1. Movements without the ball: running, jumping, cartwheels, forward and backward rolls
2. Throwing and catching different sizes and types of balls
3. Footwork through ladders
4. Passing and receiving with movement

U12 TRAINING PRIORITIES:
TRAINING TO IMPRINT SKILL AND IDEAS

When creating goalkeeping drills, activities and training sessions, it's important to begin with simple movements and gradually build up to more complex movements as improvement is seen. It doesn't make sense to have a player try to learn to move laterally to get behind the ball and smother a low shot if the player can't first save a low shot struck directly at them or if they aren't able to quickly move laterally. Just as walking must be mastered before one is able to run, movement patterns and basic catching skills must be taught before more advanced goalkeeping techniques can be mastered.

For that reason, the foundation of goalkeeper training in the early years must focus on coordination, balance and kinesthetic sense both with and without a ball. Hand-eye coordination, general movement patterns such as running backward, crossover steps and shuffling to move laterally, the drop step to move backward quickly as well as tumbling and rolling exercises on the floor to teach agility and kinesthetic sense are the vital first steps one must begin with if one eventually wants to teach a goalkeeper how to be able to move in an even more athletic way to dive for a ball lobbed over them but under the crossbar when they are older.

Another major area of focus must be to continue mastering the skills of field players, especially those that pertain to the goalkeeping position. Those skills should include short- and long-range passing, the ability to play two-touch under the pressure of time and space restrictions as well as some work on first-time clearances from the ground and air. This age group should also continue to spend some time playing games on the field and not solely in the goal to continue their understanding of the nuances of the game.

With regard to specific goalkeeping skills, the areas and principles that should be stressed are basic handling exercises where the focus is on the correct body shape to save, movement to get the body behind the ball, clean catching technique and safe diving. There should also be some emphasis on distribution skills especially in relation to a quick transition from the save to short throwing and kicking out with a focus on trying to help the team keep possession.

Examples of these types of movement and handling activities can be seen below.

Catch, throw and do footwork through sticks (top). Pass and tumble: forward or backward roll, or cart-wheel (bottom).

Different ball warm-ups.

1. Medicine ball
2. Tennis ball
3. Soccer ball

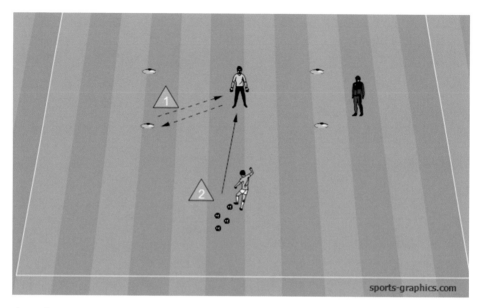

Tim Melia warm-up square (1).

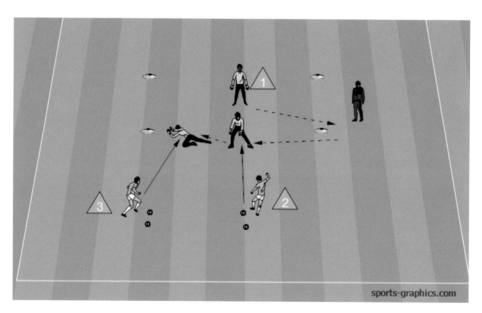

Tim Melia warm-up square (2).

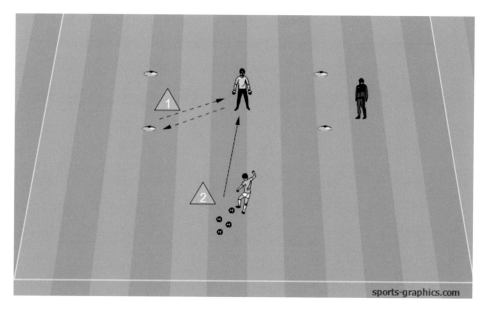

Three-shot sequence.

1. Shot on the ground
2. Volley
3. Shot on the ground

Finally, it's important to instill a passion for learning and playing the game in this age group which is done by building a relationship with your goalkeeper and focusing on the process of improvement and not on the outcome and results of games.

U13-U14/15 TRAINING PRIORITIES: TRAINING TO IMPRINT AND MASTER SKILLS AND CONCEPTS

Generally speaking, between the ages of 12-15 years, children will experience one or even multiple growth spurts. For this reason, it is vital to continue their overall athletic training so they continue to increase their coordination, balance, agility, flexibility and kinesthetic sense as their body mass, weight and height are changing. Continuing to develop these athletic characteristics will help them adapt and learn, more easily, the more specific and complex movements associated with goalkeeping during their teenage years.

Goalkeeper-specific footwork exercises to help teach how to get the body in line with shots or to track down flighted balls played over, in front of or wide of the goalkeeper are very important at this age. These footwork movements plus the balance, coordination and kinesthetic sense activities will combine to give the goalkeeper a good understanding of how his body works and moves in space allowing for more advanced techniques to save shots and crosses as he progresses and gets older.

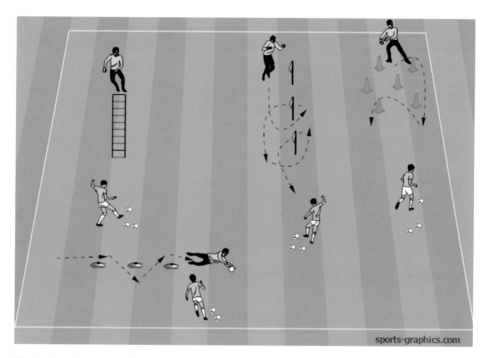

Footwork and save examples.

Footwork and save example to goal.

In addition to continuing to learn and master general and goalkeeper-specific movement patterns, they can also begin to engage in strength training, although it should start with using their own body weight. Core work, trunk stability and mobility exercises as well as various push-up and pull-up exercises will help build the strength in their muscles that will stabilize important joint capsules such as the ankles, knees, hips and shoulders of the goalkeeper. These exercises should be prescribed and monitored by a conditioning expert who is knowledgeable in the movement patterns of soccer players at the appropriate time in their physical development.

Regarding the progression of soccer- and goalkeeper-specific skills, the following guidelines will be helpful:

- Continue improving the range and accuracy of one- and two-touch passing with an emphasis on being able to play entry balls between the lines as well as being able to open up and switch play from one side to the other. These basic soccer skills will become even more important as the goalkeeper progresses to higher levels of the game and should become comfortable at this age. They should also become proficient headers of the ball as there may be times in a match where they'll need to come out of their penalty area to make clearances of flighted or bouncing balls.

- Advanced handling techniques such as diving as well as dealing with crosses can be refined at this age. The various techniques and basic tactics in dealing with through-balls and breakaways should also be an area of focus as they are becoming more aware of spatial relationships at this stage of their development.

- Much of the improvement in the diving technique as well as some of the basic understanding and movement for dealing with crosses can be done with drills and individual activities focused on the goalkeeper's movement patterns. Also, the various spreading techniques in 1-vs.-1 situations should be worked on from a technical perspective in isolated drills.

- However, the ability to deal with crosses in situations where there is pressure from the opposition as well as dealing with the timing and decision making in through-ball situations can only be improved in functional and situational exercises with both attackers and defenders present. Isolating the technical aspects from the tactical decisions is still important so that the technique doesn't break down under the pressure of reduced time, increased speed and multiple decisions that need to made in the real game. With regard to through-balls and crosses, putting the goalkeepers in small-sided games where these situations happen repeatedly is important to their continued improvement at this stage.

Example of a training environment for intermediate goalkeepers: functional and efficient.

1. Shot to save
2. Distribution to central midfielder who uncovers himself to receive
3. Back-pass from right back and distribution to the flank

3-vs.-1 functional through-ball training activity.

Dealing with crosses with multiple finishers and distribution targets for the goalkeeper.

This increased awareness of defending tactics and decision making is impossible to improve to the necessary level in isolated GK training and is a common mistake made by many coaches of goalkeepers. Therefore, training with the team in small-sided games and phase-of-play activities will help them in areas such as reading the game and helping them improve their communication and presence in the game.

Ultimately, training in these small-sided environments with the team and having the repetition and variation of situations arising with through-balls, breakaways and crowded crossing situations, the goalkeeper is exposed to moments where his courage and bravery are tested due to the possibility of physical contact. Acting instinctively in these situations, without hesitation, is developed over time in these types of training conditions and will be a big determining factor in success or failure as the goalkeeper progresses through the higher levels of the game. Like anything else, his reaction to these moments can be trained through proper age- and situational-appropriate practices and feedback.

3-vs.-3 plus two and goalkeepers emphasizes thoughtful distribution, back-passes, dealing with through-balls, and so on.

As well as teaching the more advanced and beginning tactics in defending the goal (and developing the bravery that is required for success), the goalkeepers must also begin mastering goalkeeper-specific distribution. Kicking (punting, drop-kicking and side-winders) and throwing from the hands need constant repetition and refinement to help improve consistency, accuracy and distance. The technical aspects of both throwing and kicking can once again be trained in isolation to increase proficiency but must be perfected in game-like situations so the goalkeepers can begin to understand the nuances of the timing of the distribution ("Should I play quickly or slow things down for my teammates?") as well as gaining an understanding of which players are actually open and able to receive from the goalkeeper as opposed to simply appearing to be open.

U15-U18 TRAINING PRIORITIES: TRAINING TO MASTER TECHNICAL SKILLS AND TACTICAL CONCEPTS TO COMPETE

At the older developmental ages, there should be an increased emphasis on athleticism, especially in the areas of speed, power and agility. As players physically mature into young adulthood they must continue to work at mastering all the skills mentioned previously, but now it must be done more quickly and more powerfully. Therefore, goalkeeper-specific conditioning should be included in their training regularly. This will be discussed in more detail in the chapter on fitness but suffice it to say here that plyometric work to increase power and strength in jumping motions as well as speed and quickness exercises (preferably done with a ball) need to be included in training at the appropriate time during each training week.

Plyometric: Jump and save. Jumping patterns (forward, back) and turn hurdle to do lateral work.

Plyometric: Jump, pull-up on bar, touch post, shot and save.

There must also be a continued focus on technical proficiency, especially passing and receiving over various distances. A mastery of all basic and advanced handling skills as well as distribution with the feet and hands are required at this stage. These skills can be improved and mastered with individual technique training in a solo or small group setting, but what is most important at this stage is to remember is that the goalkeeper needs to increasingly understand how his position relates to the bigger picture of team defending and transitioning into attack. Therefore, there must be increased tactical awareness and training within the team concept. To accomplish this the goalkeeper must spend even more time training with the team in group defending activities so he improves his ability to read game situations as they relate to crosses, spacing behind the defense to deal with through balls, defending set-pieces, and his ability to make the correct decision on when and how to distribute the ball once he's won it.

CHAPTER

01

CHAPTER 1

BUILDING BLOCKS: TECHNIQUE

Ready Position

The ready position is the starting point for all goalkeeper actions, from movement to shot-stopping. A sound stance gives the goalkeeper better balance, agility, power and reaction time. Many young goalkeepers develop poor habits in their basic stance that, left uncorrected, may limit their ability to reach their full potential in goal. Although subtle differences in basic stance (e.g., hand position) can be an asset for some goalkeepers, a consistent stance based on the following principles should be a constant point of coaching analysis, particularly with young keepers.

✓ Feet shoulder-width apart
✓ Weight on balls of feet

✓ Heels slightly raised

✓ Knees slightly bent, but not sitting

✓ Shoulders rolled slightly forward

✓ Head up and steady

✓ Hands at sides, off of thighs

Common corrections to a keeper's stance include the following:

✓ Feet too narrow: Limits balance and power

✓ Feet too wide: Limits movement, opens area between legs to opponents

✓ Weight on heels: Limits save range, leads to kick saves and rebounds

✓ Too erect: Limits power and ability to deal with low shots

✓ Too low: Limits ability to deal with high shots

✓ Too stiff: Slows reaction time

✓ Too lax: Prevents power and speed

MOVEMENT

Along with the basic stance, the goalkeeper's ability to move quickly and smoothly is a critical component of the technical foundation. Proper footwork speeds and makes consistent the goalkeeper's ability to control the area, save and distribute. Regular footwork and agility training makes correct movement second nature as the goalkeeper learns and refines distribution and saving techniques. It is important to recognize that there are multiple considerations in planning and training goalkeeper footwork.

✓ Shuffle. The chop step is used to move sideways while preparing to save. Shuffling footwork uses short, sharp chop steps. The feet do not come together, as this temporarily inhibits balance and makes changing directions more difficult. Also, the toes, hips and shoulders remain open to the ball throughout, allowing the goalkeeper to quickly adjust and save.

✓ Cross-over step. Explosive steps for rapid sideways movement when shuffling will not get one there in time. Cross-over steps temporarily place the goalkeeper in a position where the use of saving techniques (e.g., diving) is very difficult, and therefore not all goalkeepers and coaches use this technique. However, used in an emergency, it can allow the goalkeeper to get to a new angle quickly.

✓ Sideways run. As the term implies, the goalkeeper uses a pivot and running steps to make fast and extreme changes in angle preparation. It is important to emphasize that while the goalkeeper is running sideways, his feet, hips and shoulders are often closed to the ball, making proper saving technique extremely difficult and thus any sideways running must be accompanied by a subsequent return to the basic stance before a shot is taken.

✓ Backpedal. The goalkeeper uses backpedaling to recover toward the goal as play develops. This movement often needs to be quick and preparatory to dealing with a shot and must be conducted with a good feel for angle and depth in the area.

✓ Closing. This is forward movement to close down a shooter or tighten an angle. This movement can be accomplished through large steps (to cover ground quickly when a shot is not imminent) or short steps (when the ball is closer and a shot is imminent). Because this movement is used to tighten the space between the goalkeeper and the shooter, it is conducted with the body in the posture of the ready position, but with the hands a bit wider (making a bigger blocking area). Note: A closing movement toward a shooter ends with either a set-step, which brings the goalkeeper to the ready position (basic stance), as one cannot be moving forward and react sideways to save, or a spreading save to take the ball off of a dribbler.

Common corrections include:

✓ Feet come together while shuffling, creating a moment where balance is compromised
✓ Failure to return to ready position after movement
✓ Backpedaling without knowing one's position relative to the goal
✓ Closing using either big or small steps when the other movement is required

HANDLING

The goalkeeper uses his hands to receive and control the ball. This section examines each of the handling techniques available to the goalkeeper.

Considerations in selecting handling techniques include:

- ✓ Shot location
- ✓ Shot pace
- ✓ Weather conditions (wind, rain, extreme cold and ground conditions all influence handling technique)
- ✓ Game situation (e.g., receiving a cross in a crowded goal area).

TECHNICAL HANDLING

Standard catching: The ball is received between the base of the ribs and the top of the head.

- ✓ Position body in line with the ball.
- ✓ Starting from the ready position, raise the fingers up to face the incoming shot.
- ✓ Extend the arms to create a receiving cushion.
- ✓ Receive the ball using a "W" technique by placing the thumbs behind the ball to form the catching base.
- ✓ The eyes focus on the catch.
- ✓ Absorb the shot with the arms, demonstrating control before moving to distribute.

Common corrections:
- ✓ The body is not in line with the ball, typically resulting in poor handling.
- ✓ The keeper fails to create a "W" with the hands, creating a poor receiving base and causing drops.
- ✓ Arms are not extended to receive. Higher-paced shots will overwhelm hands and create rebounds.

Low-ball handling: The ball is received between the base of the ribs and the tops of the feet.

- ✓ Position the body in line with the ball.
- ✓ Starting from the ready position, turn the palms up and bring them to the front of the body.
- ✓ Tuck in the elbows, creating a basket with which to receive the ball.
- ✓ The eyes focus on the catch.
- ✓ Maintain slightly forward balance as the ball is absorbed.

Common corrections:

- ✓ The body is not in line with the ball. It is very difficult to catch and control in this position.
- ✓ Palms are not turned up. This common mistake leads to the ball being pushed down to the ground and a second save off of the bounce.
- ✓ Elbows are not tucked in. The ball can squeeze through and bounce off of the legs, creating a rebound.

SHORT-HOP BOUNCE

Short-hop bounce (1): Dealing with a ball that skips in front of the goalkeeper.

The ball bounces or skips right in front of the goalkeeper's feet.

✓ Position the body in line with the ball.

✓ Do not back up.

✓ From the ready position, stagger the feet slightly and angle the body forward to contain the ball as it rises.

✓ Turn the palms to face the ball.

✓ Tuck the elbows in.

✓ Keep eyes and head oriented to the ball.

✓ Maintain slightly forward balance as the ball is absorbed.

Short-hop bounce (2): Finish the save.

Common corrections:

✓ Goalkeeper backs up, creating the possibility of the attacker getting to the ball first and introducing an upright posture and handling issues.

✓ Feet are not staggered. This makes it difficult to get the proper body position (i.e., over the ball) and creates a stagnant, inflexible base from which to save.

✓ Goalkeeper traps the ball against the legs. Young goalkeepers often do this, and the ball is often not handled cleanly.

✓ Elbows are not tucked in, often resulting in rebounds off of the legs.

✓ Goalkeeper fails to keep the head and eyes oriented to the ball. Many goalkeepers keep their head and eyes up rather than on the ball in this situation, a natural aversion to the bouncing ball. Handling errors will result.

GROUND SHOTS

Ground shots: Standing.

- ✓ Position the body in line with the ball.
- ✓ Step to the ball if possible.
- ✓ Keep the feet staggered.
- ✓ Keep the palms up.
- ✓ Elbows should be tucked in behind the ball.
- ✓ Pick up the ball with both hands, stepping forward as one receives.
- ✓ Follow through, securing the ball against the rib cage between the arms with the hands secure on the ball.

Common corrections:

✓ If the ball is received to the left or right of the frame, it becomes difficult to secure the ball if hit with pace.

✓ Goalkeeper fails to move to ball, giving an attacker time to get there first.

✓ Feet are kept parallel, resulting in immobile, poor balance if contact occurs.

✓ Elbows held wide, often resulting in mishandling of the ball.

✓ Goalkeeper fails to follow through and secure the ball. The ball can be dropped with contact and distribution delayed because the goalkeeper receives the ball flat-footed.

FRONT SMOTHER

Front smother (1): Approach.

✓ Position the body in line with ball.

✓ Step to the ball if possible.

✓ Keep the feet staggered.

✓ Get low behind the ball.

✓ Elbows should be tucked in.

✓ Keep the eyes up and on the ball.

✓ Receive the ball while pushing forward along the ground behind the ball.

Front smother (2): Get behind, then under the ball.

Common corrections:

- ✓ Failure to get in line with the ball makes it difficult to control the ball if it is hit with any pace.
- ✓ Waiting on the ball allows the opponent to get to the ball first.
- ✓ Failure to stagger the feet results in no ability to push through the save.
- ✓ Staying upright too long behind the ball can allow the shot to get under the goalkeeper.
- ✓ Failure to tuck the elbows allows the ball to pass through or under the goalkeeper.
- ✓ If the eyes are not on the ball, mishandling often results.

Front smother (3): Final cover.

HIGH BALLS

High balls (1).

✓ Make the call! "Keeper!"

✓ Close with the ball as much as possible, using good footwork to move forward, sideways or back.

✓ Position the body in line with the ball.

✓ Jump from one foot, propelling the body for height and power by driving the other knee high into the jump. Arm thrust also ensures maximum jump height.

✓ Keep eyes and focus on the ball.

✓ Catch the ball at the highest possible point and in front of one's head.

✓ Land on both feet, with toes, hips and shoulders facing the direction of the arriving ball.

✓ Hold the ball high above the head until a stable landing is achieved to protect the ball in case one is contacted by another player, and to demonstrate control to the official.

High balls (2).

Common corrections:

✓ Failure to call for the ball confuses defenders and encourages opponents.

✓ Late, indecisive and inaccurate movement to the ball can result in failure to get to the ball or a contested save. Many young goalkeepers fail to take the proper angle to the ball (direct) and leave late to arrive on time.

✓ Poor jumping and landing form is often a result of a poor approach angle, failure to push through the jump or poor physical agility.

✓ Catching the ball too low and late can result in an interception by an attacker while catching it behind one's eyesight, often creates drops or goals.

✓ Bringing the ball down during landing can result in a loss of control and questions from the official as to whether the goalkeeper ever established control.

Catching at the bar.

This is a distinctive, important save for young goalkeepers in particular. Whereas the standard high ball save described above typically involves dealing with a cross or fielding a ball served into traffic where the goalkeeper has to go and get the ball, catching at the bar refers to a shot on goal that will go in below the bar. The goalkeeper can tip the ball, but catching is preferred if possible.

✓ Retreat to within a step of the goal line if possible.
✓ Position the body in line with the ball.
✓ Jump with both feet, keeping the toes, hips and shoulders facing the field and the angle from which the shot is coming.
✓ Eyes and focus should be on the ball throughout the save.
✓ Catch the ball in front of and above one's head.
✓ Focus on making a stable landing with feet, hips, shoulders facing the field and angle of the shot.

Common corrections:
✓ Goalkeeper fails to get near the goal line before setting to save.
✓ Goalkeeper tries to jump and save outside of his body frame.

✓ Jumping from one foot or with the body twisted can result in a limited jump and drops or misses.

✓ Goalkeeper fails to fix his attention on the ball.

✓ Catching the ball behind one's eyesight or with one hand typically results in drops or goals.

✓ A twisted or off-balance landing often results in rebounds.

DIVING

Diving.

The most exciting and most difficult saves for goalkeepers often involve diving, from dealing with shots to corners to emergency reaction saves that demand great reach. Diving is a combination of quick footwork, body placement and handling. There are several types of dive and other saves (e.g., blocking) that are extensions of the diving technique. It is paramount that younger goalkeepers first learn safe, proper diving technique before experimenting with more explosive dives.

Collapse dive (1): Approach.

This save is used for low shots that cannot be dealt with from a standing position. The goalkeeper typically uses this save to corral a ball hit with pace and slightly outside of his frame.

✓ Position the body slightly off line with ball.

✓ Begin from the ready position with the weight on the front portion of the feet.

✓ Step toward the ball and forward with the near-side foot.

✓ Proper dive angle: Dive forward (not sideways or backward) to get to the ball sooner and maximize the angle.

✓ The near-side knee bends and goes to ground (outside of knee contacts ground) followed by the hip and outside of the shoulder. It is important that the goalkeeper not roll backward or forward on landing.

✓ When possible, keep the eyes in line with the ball.

✓ Near-side hand should be on the back of the ball with the other hand on top. Use the ground as a third hand.

✓ Hold the ball in line with the eyes (and about a foot away), with the elbows slightly bent.

✓ The bottom leg should be nearly straight; the trailing leg should be bent at the knee for protection and faster recoil after the save.

Collapse dive (2): Going to ground.

Common corrections:

- ✓ Goalkeeper is positioned straight-on with the ball, causing hesitation and poor form.
- ✓ Failure to step in the direction of the dive limits the range of the dive and can contribute to an improper, negative dive angle.
- ✓ Inexperienced goalkeepers tend to use improper contact points (e.g., they land on their elbows) which can cause physical damage over time and limits the ability to control the ball.
- ✓ Failure to establish proper hand position leads to rebounds and missed saves.
- ✓ Holding the ball above or below eye height can lead to loss of control.
- ✓ Goalkeeper uses improper leg position. If the top leg is straight, it leads to poor recoil, and can contribute to the goalkeeper rolling on their back and failure to protect oneself.

Collapse dive (3): Finish the save.

Extension diving (1): Explosive push to the ball.

Extension diving is an emergency save used to deal with shots hit with heavy pace and beyond the reach of a collapse dive save.

✓   Begin from the ready position with the weight on the front portion of the feet.

✓   Step toward the ball and forward with the near-side foot.

✓ Use an explosive push from the near-side foot.

✓ For a low shot: The near-side knee bends and goes to ground (outside of the knee contacts the ground) followed by the hip and outside of the shoulder.

✓ For a shot in the air: Extend the body, pushing through the air to meet the ball.

✓ When possible, keep the eyes in line with the ball.

✓ Near-side hand should be on the back of the ball with the trailing hand on top (bringing the ball to the ground).

✓ Hold the ball in line with the eyes (and about a foot away), with elbows slightly bent.

✓ The bottom leg should be nearly straight; the trailing leg should be bent at the knee for protection and faster recoil after the save.

Extension diving (2): Finish the save.

Common corrections:

- ✓ Failure to step in the direction of the dive limits the range of the dive and can contribute to improper, negative dive angle. Extension diving requires power, and the goalkeeper must push through the save.
- ✓ Inexperienced goalkeepers tend to use improper contact points (e.g., they land on their elbows), which can cause physical damage over time and limits the ability to control the ball.
- ✓ Do not over-dive. There is a tendency among new extension divers to want to fly through the air. Make the simplest save possible, and avoid injuries and rebounds.
- ✓ Failure to establish proper hand position leads to rebounds and missed saves.
- ✓ Ball held above or below eye height can lead to loss of control.
- ✓ Goalkeeper uses improper leg position. If the top leg is straight, it leads to poor recoil, and can contribute to the goalkeeper rolling on their back and failure to protect oneself.

SPREADING

Spreading.

This technique is used in 1-vs.-1 situations where the goalkeeper has to block an opponent approaching the goal, or cover a contested ball in the area. The approach and application of the save will be examined more closely in the tactical chapter, but it must be emphasized that this technique is to be employed when the goalkeeper has closed with the attacker and the ball.

- ✓ Approach the ball and the attacker.
- ✓ Get slightly off center to facilitate spreading behind the ball.
- ✓ Think in terms of getting on the ball as early as possible.
- ✓ Get into the opponent's feet if you will arrive after that player at the ball.
- ✓ Reach the hands to the ball as early as possible.
- ✓ Contact points on the dive are outside of the knees, outside of the hip and shoulder.
- ✓ Trailing (back-side) hand and leg start high to block and then the hand closes on the top of the ball.
- ✓ Note the position of the near-side hand at the back of the ball and the extended but bent lower arm. This position allows the goalkeeper to absorb some pressure on the ball without injury or rebound.
- ✓ Note that the ball is held, ideally, in line with the eyes.
- ✓ The body is spread across the goal, and a slight scissor motion at the hips at the moment of the save can help contain the ball and limit an attacker's options.

Common corrections:
- ✓ Goalkeeper comes straight on to ball and drops to his knees rather than spreading before goal. This can lead to injuries and leaves the goalkeeper in a poor defending position.
- ✓ Goalkeeper leads with their feet, rather than their hands. This is an indication that the goalkeeper is scared and has shifted his weight to his heels. This error produces, at best, rebounds, and at worst, fouls and penalty kicks.
- ✓ Failure to get into the opponent's feet. Going down too far from the opponent and the ball leaves the goalkeeper vulnerable to being dribbled or chipped.
- ✓ Goalkeeper fails to close up around the ball. If there is a rebound, the goalkeeper may be unable to control it or prevent the attacker pushing the ball in behind him.

K-stop.

This is an increasingly popular variation of spreading used to block an attempt from an attacker in tight to the goal. Attackers frequently anticipate a goalkeeper going to ground and spreading and therefore will nick a ball in the air to go over the goalkeeper. The K-stop combats this problem by leaving the goalkeeper in the upright position, prepared to knock down balls played above the point covered by spreading. In the photo above, the goalkeeper has gotten close and dropped to one knee, with his arms spread to block the shot (see the "K" outlined by his body position).

✓ Get tight to the attacker.
✓ Use this save in situations near the goal (e.g., a cut-back cross), and not typically in a breakaway situation.
✓ Drop to one knee.
✓ Arms are out to block shots.
✓ Recover quickly to one's feet, as a rebound is likely in this situation.

TIPPING

Used in an emergency to deal with a ball that cannot be caught, tipping involves extending the body to push the ball beyond the frame of the goal. Goalkeepers tip balls hit with pace that's too heavy to handle cleanly; shots that require a quick reaction (e.g., a shot tipped in front of them); shots that they cannot reach with both hands to catch; shots or crosses that have to be dealt with in a crowded goal box; or shots that, due to wet or windy conditions, are too dangerous to try to catch. In every case, goalkeepers should be encouraged to catch the ball if at all possible, as a tip often creates a corner kick for the opposition.

Low tipping

✓ Begin from the ready position with the weight on the front portion of the feet.

✓ Step toward the ball and forward with the near-side foot.

✓ Dive forward (not sideways or backward) to get to the ball sooner and maximize angle.

✓ The near-side knee bends and goes to ground (outside of knee contacts ground) followed by the hip and outside of shoulder. It is important that the goalkeeper not roll backward or forward on landing.

✓ When possible, keep the eyes in line with the ball.

✓ Extend the near-side, lower hand to meet and absorb the weight of the shot.

✓ Contact point is either the boney, base of the palm (power), or the base of the fingers (better feel and control).

✓ The arm bends with the ball and then extends to push the ball wide of the frame. Ideally, the ball is pushed along the end line, rather than over it and out for a corner.

✓ Eyes travel with the ball throughout the save.

✓ Top (back-side) leg is bent for protection and better recoil after the save.

Common corrections:

✓ Failure to step in the direction of the dive limits the range of the dive and can contribute to an improper, negative dive angle. Extension diving requires power, and the goalkeeper must push through the save.

✓ Inexperienced goalkeepers tend to use improper contact points (e.g., they land on their elbows), which can cause physical damage over time and limits the ability to control the ball.

✓ Do not over-dive. There is a tendency among new extension divers to want to fly through the air. Make the simplest save possible, and avoid injuries and mistakes.

✓ Failure to extend the hand to meet the ball creates difficulty controlling and redirecting the ball.

✓ Inexperienced goalkeepers tend to get the ball stuck underneath their hand as they tip. This is the result of rolling the hand over the ball and trapping it against the ground. Encourage the goalkeeper to push the pinky finger side of their hand along the ground even before the save, establishing contact behind the ball.

✓ Often failure to be strong with the fingers will lead to a ball going behind the goalkeeper and not traveling away from the goal. A strong hand posture and a determined push are necessary to put the ball well away from goal.

High tipping

✓ Learn this skill from a kneeling position to start (see above) to remove the footwork and focus on the hand movement.

✓ Goalkeeper must get shoulder-on (point one shoulder at the server and ball), and use the hand closest to the server to tip.

✓ Point the wrist of the tipping hand at the server and ball. This wrist must remain locked in orientation throughout the save.

✓ Bend the arm at the elbow and receive the ball with an absorbing motion.

✓ Contact point on the hand is the base of the fingers (control) or, less desirably, the base of the hand (power, but difficult to control shots not hit with a lot of pace).

✓ Push the ball above and in front of the head (eyes travel with the ball).

✓ Follow through in the direction of the bar, keeping the wrist oriented toward the field.

✓ Lift with the fingers to assure the ball travels well over the bar.

✓   Add the footwork. The goalkeeper starts on his line (above). The server stands 6 yards from goal.

✓   The goalkeeper moves out and touches the ball. Note the drop-step that is the keeper's first movement toward goal. This step closes the shoulders of the goalkeeper to the ball, indicating the tipping hand (right hand in the photo).

✓ Goalkeeper finishes the tip, propelling the ball over the bar. Note the concentration on the ball, the proper wrist orientation and the ball contact.

✓ Common corrections:

✓ The most common error in technical execution is the goalkeeper turning his wrist to face the goal. Because of the natural downward rotation of the arm, the goalkeeper can throw the ball right into the goal, and the ability to lift the ball is very limited.

✓ Eyes must be on the ball throughout. Young goalkeepers worry about running into the netting and any miscalculation here can result in a poor tip.

✓ Failure to close the shoulders to the ball while recovering to goal makes the tip much more difficult. Again, the drop-step helps to prevent this situation. If a goalkeeper keeps his shoulders open or opens them while backpedaling, he loses any sense of his location vis-à-vis the goal, and it becomes extremely difficult to gain lift and power on the tip.

✓ Many goalkeepers need time and training to develop good touch with their fingers. As a consequence, inexperienced goalkeepers will have balls roll off of their fingers and drop, or strike the base of the palm and ricochet. Frequent training from the kneeling position outlined above will correct this tendency.

✓ It is imperative that the goalkeeper become proficient at tipping with both hands, as situations will demand the ability to tip under duress on both sides.

PUNCHING

Punching progression, with the goalkeeper isolating the skill by working from a seated position.

The preference is always to catch the ball and young goalkeepers in particular must be urged to use punching in emergency situations. Those moments include crosses, balls dealt with in a crowded area, adverse weather conditions (e.g., wind, rain), or a ball hit with too much pace to be held.

- ✓ Position the body in line with the ball.
- ✓ Form fists. Do not tuck the thumb inside the fist!
- ✓ Hold the fists near your chest.
- ✓ Play as early as possible by moving toward the ball. Jumping from one foot and propelling oneself through the ball will add power to the punch.
- ✓ The fists are prepared by holding them slightly apart, just enough to broaden the contact area.
- ✓ Push the fists through the lower half of the ball, as a lower contact point will cause the ball to sail higher and limit the possibility of the ball ricocheting off of another player.

- ✓ Ideally, punch the ball (1) high, (2) wide and (3) far, in that order.
- ✓ Follow through with the punch to full extension of the arms to gain maximum power in the punch.

Common corrections:

- ✓ Punching outside of the width of one's frame will limit power and accuracy.
- ✓ Failure to form and hold fists is common among young goalkeepers and will lead to punching that does not propel the ball over distance.
- ✓ If power is missing from the punches, demonstrate the importance of holding the fists close to the chest as one prepares to punch, thereby extending the punching push.
- ✓ If the contact is higher on the ball, the punch will send the ball down or at a flat trajectory, creating close-in rebounds.
- ✓ If the goalkeeper fails to follow through, extending the arms, then the punch will also fail to travel over distance.

High tipping: Side shot.

This is a simple means of pushing the ball over the bar from wide-angle shots that make use of the up-field hand difficult.

- ✓ Get near the line with the body open to the ball.
- ✓ Use the hand nearest the goal to tuck the ball over the bar, being careful to use the fingers to emphasize lift on the ball to avoid pushing the ball into the goal.

OR

- ✓ Use the up-field hand to carry the ball over the bar for shots and crosses on that side of the body.

Common corrections:
- ✓ If the goalkeeper is not open to the ball, it can be difficult to turn the ball over the bar.
- ✓ The palm is useful for absorbing the pace of the serve, but the fingers provide control and lift.

BOXING

Boxing practiced in pairs, with the players knocking the ball back and forth with alternating hands.

Similar to punching, boxing uses one hand to punch the ball away from the goal in an emergency situation. Boxing is used when the ball cannot be caught. Deflections, weather conditions (e.g., wind, rain), a crowded box area, balls hit with heavy pace from in close that cannot be caught and so on all call for a boxing save. Be certain to train to box the ball with either hand.

✓   Position the body in line with the ball if possible.
✓   Form a fist. Do not tuck the thumb inside the fist!
✓   Bring the fist close to the body, ideally near chest height.
✓   Box through the bottom half of the ball to propel the ball up and away from the goal area.
✓   Follow through, extending the fist to create power in the boxing save.

Common corrections:
✓   Fist is not tight. Ball will not travel far from goal.
✓   Fist is extended when boxing action starts, resulting in a ball that does not leave the area.
✓   Boxing through the high back of the ball will push the ball down, creating a rebound in the area and possibly deflections in behind the goalkeeper.
✓   Failure to follow through will limit the power of the boxing save.

DISTRIBUTION

There are two forms of distribution: thrown and rolled. Goalkeepers must become proficient distributing the ball cleanly both by underhand roll and throwing. In general, distributing by hand is quick and accurate, increasing the team's ability to move forward in possession.

Rolling is used for quick, short distribution, typically to one of the back line players.

Rolled distribution (1).

- ✓ Assess the situation. If the target player can turn, play his front foot or lead him to facilitate movement forward.
- ✓ Similar to bowling, cup the ball in the rolling hand.
- ✓ Reach the fingers of the rolling hand down toward the ground during the release motion.
- ✓ Step with the foot opposite the rolling hand during the rolling motion.
- ✓ Release the ball at the bottom of the arm motion.
- ✓ Finish with the rolling hand low to prevent bounce in the service.

Rolled distribution (2).

Common corrections:
- ✓ For young goalkeepers, there is a tendency to want to use two hands to hold the ball. Use a smaller ball if needed for teaching this skill.
- ✓ Releasing the ball too early creates a bounce that is hard to receive and also takes pace off of the distribution.
- ✓ Failure to reach down to release creates a bouncing serve that is hard to receive.
- ✓ If released too late, the ball will travel through the air and be difficult to receive.

SKIPPED

Skipped pass distribution: Side-arm throw that pushes the fingers down to create backspin.

This throw is used for mid-distance distribution. Skip passes can be thrown with more pace and over more distance than rolled passes. They also skid or bounce and can be harder to control.

- ✓ Cup the ball with the throwing hand, holding the ball near the shoulder.
- ✓ Step with the opposite side foot as you complete the throwing motion.
- ✓ Drop the throwing shoulder to lessen the angle of release, limiting bounce.
- ✓ Hold the bottom, back half of the ball.
- ✓ Push the hand forward through the bottom half of the ball, attempting to push down toward the ground with the fingers (create back spin, which lessens bounce).
- ✓ Follow through low and observe the backspin on the ball.
- ✓ Throw the ball about half of the distance to the target in the air, allowing the skip to help the ball settle down for the receiving player.

Common corrections:

✓ The ball is not held using the palm and fingers on the back and bottom of the ball, leading to inconsistent, poorly controlled throws.

✓ The throwing shoulder is held high. The ball will travel at a higher trajectory, creating more bounce and a tougher pass to control.

✓ No backspin is created. The ball will bounce higher, making the pass harder to control.

✓ Throwing the ball at the ground creates a pass that bounces and likely arrives late to the target.

✓ Throwing the ball too far in the air makes extra work for the receiving player, as the pass will be bouncing or still in the air.

THROWING

Throwing (1): Preparation.

Used for distributing the ball accurately over distance, this pass travels in the air most or all of the distance to the target. The pass should generally be as flat and hard as possible, to maximize time saved and allow the team to move forward in possession.

✓ The ball is cupped in the hand and pressed against the inside of the wrist (more surface contact creates more control).

✓ The movement is similar to throwing a baseball.

✓ Stride forward with the non-throwing side foot during the throwing motion.

✓ The throwing arm remains locked throughout the throwing motion.

✓ Use the non-throwing arm to create balance.

✓ Shift the weight from the back foot to the front foot during the throwing motion.

✓ Bring the ball over the top of the shoulder, learning to find the proper release point to get the ball on target.

Throwing (2). Note the extension of the throwing arm, which will help create power and consistency in the throw. Also important here is the shift of weight from the back to the front foot as the goalkeeper moves the ball forward.

Throwing (3).

Common corrections:

- ✓ For young goalkeepers, cupping the ball and keeping the arm straight are difficult aspects of the throwing action. Try using a smaller ball to outline and gain comfort with the technique.
- ✓ Bending the throwing arm limits the force garnered to throw and creates targeting issues as the throw becomes less predictable.
- ✓ Throwing sidearm is the most common issue for developing goalkeepers. Throwing sidearm can create some power, but it also leads to targeting issues, as the long arc of potential release points means there will be balls thrown across a wider trajectory than would be the case with the ball brought over the top of the shoulder.
- ✓ Release too early and the ball flies high in the air.
- ✓ Release too late and the ball travels too low to the ground.

PLAYING WITH ONE'S FEET

Dating back to the change in the back-pass rule a generation ago, the goalkeeper position has evolved tactically to the point where he must be proficient playing from the ground with both feet and under pressure. The goalkeeper's ability to punt or drop kick also gives the team the opportunity to stretch the field immediately when the goalkeeper gains possession.

PASSING

The goalkeeper must be able to be the starting point for the attack and also a supporting player in possession. Goalkeepers therefore develop strong short passing skills with both feet, including the ability to play under pressure.

Long passing.

Driven, lofted and chipped passes over distance should be regular training topics for intermediate and advanced goalkeepers. Whether distributing to start the attack or clearing in an emergency, the ability to play the ball over distance is an important goalkeeper asset. These passes will also allow the goalkeeper to take his own goal kicks, which permits the team to take a more aggressive stance for these restarts.

PUNTING

Punting (1): Service.

Again, the ability to play over distance and with accuracy forces the opposition to defend deeper and allows the team to take a more advanced posture when the goalkeeper distributes with a punt. This skill should be practiced regularly, and with an emphasis on control and consistency.

✓ Hold the ball about waist height. Young goalkeepers tend to want to use both hands to hold and release the ball, which is fine to start, but is a habit that needs to be broken for specialists, as it limits range.

✓ Turn the hips slightly to the kicking leg side, as this creates a more natural approach and power follow-through, and makes it easier to release the ball consistently onto the punting foot.

✓ Develop a consistent footwork pattern for punting. Most goalkeepers use three steps to punt, but others find fewer or more steps useful. Regardless, the crucial concept is that the footwork sets a predictable and powerful base for kicking.

✓ Release the ball and kick with the laces, following through in the direction of the target.

✓ Control the height with the striking point. In other words, striking the ball just before it hits the ground will lead to a low trajectory, whereas a high striking point will send the ball on a high flight.

✓ Follow-through. Some advanced goalkeepers use a scissor motion with the legs (land on the kicking foot after powering through the ball) to add force to their punting. Others do not and still achieve considerable distance. It's a matter of personal preference and what is effective.

✓ It is noteworthy that some goalkeepers prefer a side-winding technique, which allows for plenty of power while also keeping the ball on a flat trajectory (which gets the ball to the target very quickly). To hit the ball this way, turn the hips more sharply to the kicking leg side, serve the ball wider with the hands and bring the kicking foot along at a higher, flatter, wider angle.

✓ Another variation of the punt is the drop kick. This type of kick also allows for a lower, more direct trajectory. Here, the ball is dropped and allowed to hit the ground and is struck using the laces as it rises. Proper timing and consistent delivery are mandatory elements of this technique.

Punting (2): Follow through.

Training punting by kicking balls into the goal, which makes for efficient practice and allows for close attention to technique.

Common corrections:

- ✓ Varied hand service leads to inconsistent form.
- ✓ Some goalkeepers approach the ball with a straight-on footwork and body pattern. The result is rigid, awkward-looking punts that are often short and high. The angled approach allows the goalkeeper to move through the ball in a more flowing, powerful manner.
- ✓ Early strike points result in ground balls and low punts while late strike points result in looping, high punts.
- ✓ Shanking the ball is a result of not striking the ball evenly but hitting inside or outside of center. Observe the spin on the ball which indicates where the ball was struck, and correct this tendency through training.
- ✓ Lack of power is often attributable to failure to lock the leg below the hip when striking or a lack of follow-through (the leg stops on contact instead of pushing through the ball).
- ✓ There are many potential causes for inaccuracy, including all of the above. Another contributing factor can be the direction of the follow-through. Some goalkeepers swing powerfully across their bodies and in so doing create an awkward motion that makes for inconsistent delivery. Others simply need to train on the topic more frequently to refine technique.

CHAPTER

02

CHAPTER 2

GETTING THERE: GOALKEEPER FITNESS

GOALKEEPER FITNESS

Physical periodization is the systematic planning of physical training involving progressive cycling of various aspects of a training program during a specific period. *Periodization* is a fancy term for planning, by which a training plan or soccer season is divided into smaller, easy-to-manage segments that are typically referred to as phases of training. In a team sport like soccer, these phases may include pre-season, in-season, post-season or play-offs, and off-season. Physical periodization involves planning and structuring within these training phases to target specific biomotor abilities (i.e., strength, power and speed) as well as position-specific skills performed by the goalkeeper.

Tactical periodization is the systematic planning of tactical training. The goal is to reach the best possible performance in the most important competitions of the season. This concept involves cycling various aspects of a training program during the season.

A *training cycle* is a series of steps or stages that make up a complete training program. The macro cycle entails the entire season and is your annual plan. A micro cycle is the period between games (usually a week) facilitating a focused block of training. A general approach to planning used by coaches during a soccer season is to plan the upcoming week of training based on the result from their team's previous match and on the upcoming opponent. This typically occurs within a smaller, seven-day training phase (Monday through Sunday), which is referred to as a micro cycle by sports science practitioners, but can simply be termed the training week.

Training stimulus is the prescribed training that induces physiological changes in the human body. Variables used to manipulate the training stimulus are intensity, duration, frequency and volume in regards to the amount and type of work placed on the body.

Another important concept for planning the training week is to prescribe an appropriate *training load*. The term *training load* has become a buzzword in both the soccer and sports science communities. Training load entails measuring the prescribed physical work completed by an athlete (i.e., external load) and the accompanying physiological or perceptual response of the athlete (i.e., internal load). The individual characteristics of an athlete (e.g., chronological age, training age, injury history and physical capacity) combined with the applied external and internal training loads determine the training outcome. For example, a goalkeeper training session involving four athletes performing identical exercises of equal repetitions could elicit considerably different internal training loads in the four athletes due to their vastly different individual characteristics.

INTRODUCTION

One can argue about what may be the most important physical characteristics necessary to succeed as a goalkeeper or how to achieve the best training stimulus when trying to improve one of those characteristics. The one thing that cannot be argued is that being in the best possible condition gives a player the best opportunity for success.

The physical requirements for a goalkeeper are different from those of field players. Therefore, it's important to understand the physical requirements of a player undertaking the goalkeeping position. Anaerobic fitness and explosive power—used in diving and jumping movements—won't make a goalkeeper taller, but it will certainly help him jump higher. Increased speed, agility and reactions used on every action and movement a goalkeeper executes when saving shots won't make one move like Michael Jackson on the dance floor, but it will certainly aid one in defending the goal against the opposition's most vicious shots and crosses. Finally, increasing upper body strength may not give one the body of Adonis, but it will certainly help the goalkeeper get off the ground more quickly after diving to deflect a shot he couldn't hold onto initially.

Therefore, improving the physical attributes of a goalkeeper has its place in the overall training program. The objective of this chapter is to incorporate physical training into training sessions, and make it specific to the game and the actions that the goalkeeper makes.

This chapter first explains the reasoning behind periodization. From there, this section delves into the requirements of a goalkeeper and the energy systems that he most often uses and how that differs from field players. Finally, the chapter discusses how to apply these to a weekly micro cycle when preparing training sessions for the goalkeeper.

Periodization begins from a physical platform. Coaches who work within a tactical periodization framework would argue otherwise; however, many of them would concede that the exercises they are creating to work on their particular team's game model must be plugged into the appropriate days of the training cycle, otherwise their players will suffer the consequence of too little recovery and too much fatigue on game day.

Therefore, regardless of which form of periodization you prefer, physical or tactical, as a coach you must first decide which energy systems are most important for your players to train on that day and whether they will have enough time to recover from them by game day. Only then can you consider anything else regarding activities and drills in your training session. This must be applied not only to field players and teams but goalkeepers as well.

The fact that exercises and training activities must occur at specific points in the training cycle doesn't mean this should be the only consideration that a coach gives to one's weekly periodization. One should, as stressed by the followers of tactical periodization, give consideration to the areas of the game that the goalkeeper must improve, then fit those activities into the proper sequence and into the proper day to ensure the correct training stimulus as well as an adequate amount of recovery time before the next match.

When training a team, anaerobic training sessions as well as aerobic high-, moderate- and low-intensity sessions can be planned in accordance with the next match and the recovery time needed so that the players are in peak physical condition for each game. While some of the physical qualities and actions required of the goalkeeper are similar to those required by field players, the energy systems most used by the goalkeeper are different. As opposed to the field players, the goalkeeper's actions are usually brief but intense bouts of maximum effort including sprinting over 5- to 15-yard distances, jumping, diving and immediately getting off the ground to face a follow-up action, throwing and kicking the ball. These actions may last only a few seconds at a time but are repeated often throughout the match. Therefore, goalkeepers require a different type of focus physically and different training activities from the rest of the team to produce the specific adaptations that will improve their game.

THE ENERGY SYSTEMS

The body produces energy primarily through three systems based on the duration of the activity and its intensity: the aerobic system, the anaerobic-alactic system and the anaerobic-lactic system. When analyzing the energy requirements of the goalkeeper position, all three systems are used to some degree. However, the most important energy system is the anaerobic-alactic system, which is responsible for explosive power. The anaerobic-alactic system works without oxygen for roughly 5-15 seconds without producing lactic acid, hence the name. Because this system works without producing lactic acid (waste products that produce fatigue in the muscles), it can quickly recover, usually in less than 60 seconds. Although this is the most important energy system for the goalkeeper, it is not the only one and, even more importantly, cannot be trained too often during the weekly micro cycle without producing too much fatigue and hindering performance. With any form of training there is a cumulative effect of fatigue that the coaches must guard against so that the players can function optimally come game day. Therefore, we must first understand the amount of recovery time the body requires when focusing on each energy system and then insert those types of training days into the appropriate spot in the weekly training calendar.

For example, the body can recover from low to moderate aerobic work within roughly 24 hours. More intense aerobic activities usually necessitate 24-48 hours to recover. Anaerobic training usually requires 72-96 hours of recovery. That's not to say that your players can't train at all in that window of recovery time, it just means that they should try not to over-stress or emphasize that same energy system during that recovery window.

PHYSICAL REQUIREMENTS OF THE GOALKEEPING POSITION

Speed, strength, quickness and power! Although necessary to some degree in all soccer positions and most sports, these physical attributes are the physical and technical cornerstone for a goalkeeper's actions.

The nature and physical requirements of the goalkeeper position have been taken into account there are a few other factors to consider. The length of the season, the number of training sessions per week, the miles and time it takes to travel to and from a match, the number of days between matches and finally the amount of time necessary for recovery from certain types of sessions are all important things to consider when building one's training cycle for the week.

When periodization is done correctly, players will be at their peak performance level for each game, and there is also a layering effect that takes place, allowing the players to achieve increasing levels of fitness (as well as skill and tactical understanding) as the season goes along. This also creates a situation where their optimum fitness levels are achieved late in the season (when the games are most important) without losing freshness. If done incorrectly, the players will suffer from overtraining and hit a physical wall, and performance decreases as the season progresses.

In summary, as a coach, you must combine the scientific principles of physical periodization with the conceptual and tactical ideas you want to get across to the goalkeeper. When combining these, you create efficient training sessions that are physically, technically and tactically integrated.

The following is a look at what a generic training cycle may look like with one game per week when combining the concepts of both physical and tactical periodization.

THE WEEKLY MICRO CYCLE

Saturday: Game

Sunday: Off (Variation: Sunday regeneration with Monday off)

The regeneration session following a match could take place the day following the match or two days later. Science shows 24-48 hours after the match is the correct window of time in which to perform this regeneration training. However, we have found—through experiences at both the youth and professional level—that players are not quite ready to focus with any intensity the day immediately following a match. Most players, especially in the professional game, need some time to get away and emotionally detach from the game especially since travel and an inability to sleep deeply can affect many players after a match. With this in mind, to keep from heaping even more physical stress on their bodies, it's best to give the day following a match off, although, as mentioned earlier, it is scientifically appropriate to do it either day.

Monday: Regeneration and Recovery Training

On the first day back from the game, the session should consist of aerobic low- to moderate-intensity training with some very short high-intensity bursts for recovery and regeneration. Provided the body doesn't endure bouts of intense work for long periods of time, therefore inducing fatigue through the build-up of lactic acid, it will recover from this type of session within 24 hours. This session could include things like continuous passing activities to work on passing and receiving as well as switching play out of the back. It should also include movement and handling activities. Although it's appropriate to vary the intensity of the work physically—as stated earlier there should be some short bursts of intense activity lasting 5-10 seconds—it would not be advisable to have many activities with a lot of mental and cognitive involvement. The simpler the activity the better on a regeneration day. Let the body do the work it needs to aid the recovery

process and let the mind rest for the more stressful and complicated work to be done later in the week.

The following diagrams give some ideas of simple passing and handling activities that would be appropriate for a regeneration session. There are many variations on these and you are only limited by your imagination and the intensity and duration of the exercise (which should be relatively low for recovery purposes).

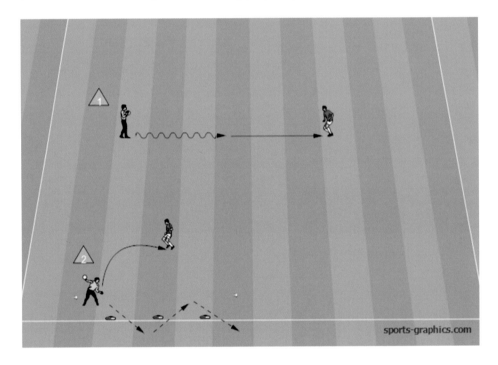

Goalkeeper warm-up with footwork and kinesthetic sense.

1. Dribble, pass, forward roll
2. Throw followed by footwork

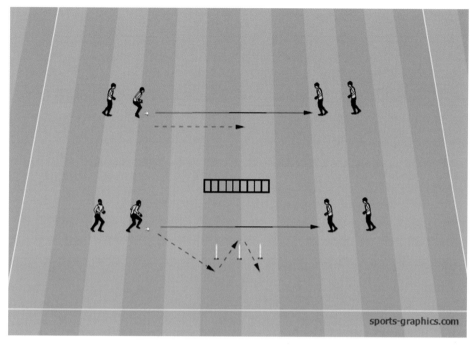

Passing and handling in lines and with footwork.

Footwork and handling.

Tuesday: Goalkeeper-Specific Power

Once the body has had some time to recover (and the mind has some time to relax), it is appropriate to train the most important energy system to the goalkeeper: the anaerobic-alactic system. The reason it is so important to the goalkeeper's performance is because it is responsible for the quick bursts of action and explosiveness so commonly seen in goalkeeper saves and distribution. However, its importance shouldn't be overemphasized by training this system too often during the week (one session per week is sufficient) or for too long during a practice session.

This anaerobic type of training, with its explosive movements, mimics the actions of a game from which the body will fully recover in 72-96 hours. One of the most important aspects of this type of training is the maximum intensity involved and its very short duration (5 seconds or less).

Below are a few exercises that are very short in duration and can be done at both maximum speed and maximum strength to elicit the training stimulus sought when training the anaerobic-alactic system for power.

sports-graphics.com

Power-diving exercise.

- Goalkeeper begins on his right side.
- At a command from the coach, he pops up and power-dives to his left, where the ball is shot.

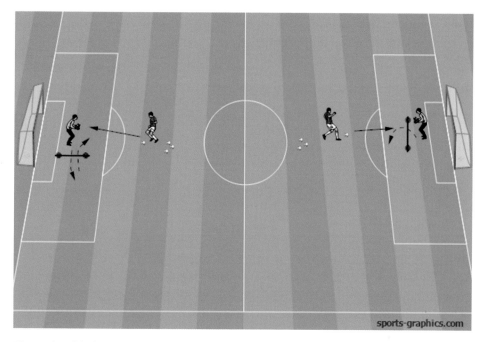

Plyometrics with shooting.

Wednesday: Low-Intensity Functional Training

The day following the power session should be a functional training session and should not be anaerobic in nature. These activities could be continuous in nature or use shorter bursts of activity provided they are not of maximum effort. This session should be structured to work more on the decisions that goalkeepers have to make ("Should I come off my line or stay? Should I catch or punch? Where should my starting position be as the ball changes from one area of the field to another?"), rather than built around a physical foundation or energy system.

Although most goalkeeping drills and activities should be done in a goal, the regeneration session, with its various types of movement and handling exercises, and the power session, with all the explosive jumping and saving, could be done in an area of the field that doesn't destroy the grass in the goalmouth. However, on these functional days it's extremely important to work in the goal so that the goalkeeper has to move and make decisions based on his positioning and the ball and opponent's position relative to the goal.

As stated above, these types of training days are based around decision making and it's most productive if that can be done in the realistic environment of playing in a goal with the proper six-yard box and penalty area markings.

Below are some examples of functional activities and drills that one could incorporate into this type of session.

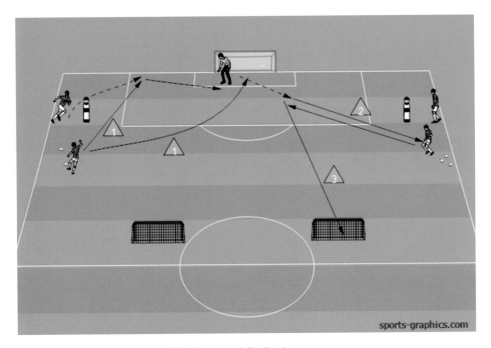

Functional three-goal situation with back-pass and distribution.

1. Deal with short cross or serve to back half of goal (server's choice).
2. Distribute wide, receive back-pass and play forward to target goal.
3. Repeat in the other direction.

Functional three-goal and through-ball activities.

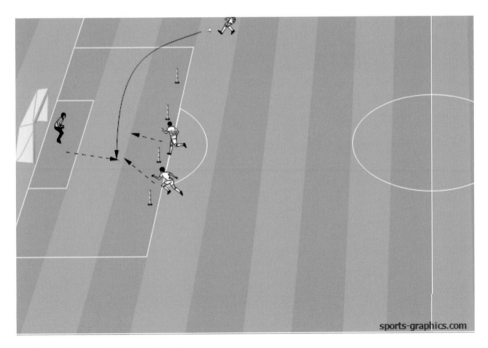

Dealing with serves behind the back four.

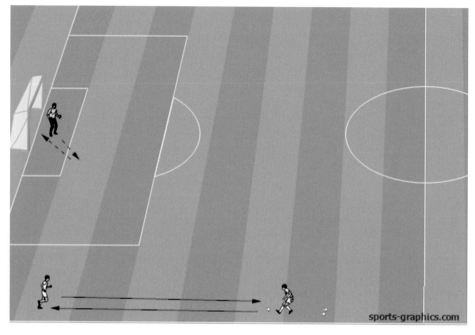

Adjusting starting position on various wide service positions.

Thursday: Speed of Actions

When we talk about speed of action, we aren't referring to straight line speed or even necessarily talking about pure running speed at all. It refers to the speed in which we can complete a soccer action that is specific to the position of the goalkeeper. This match-related, specificity of training is a principle that must be adhered to if you actually want to reap the benefits of improved movement speed as it relates to playing the actual game.

These exercises and drills should be 5-20 seconds in duration and the energy system being used during these actions is the anaerobic-alactic system. The difference between this type of training day and a power day is the lack of maximum muscle contractions and repeated explosiveness in the exercises. Here are some example activities you can use to train specific speed.

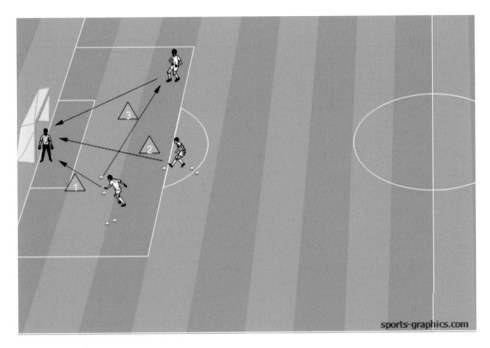

Three-shot session.

1. Turn and save.
2. Volley.
3. Track cross and save.

Footwork agility and shot.

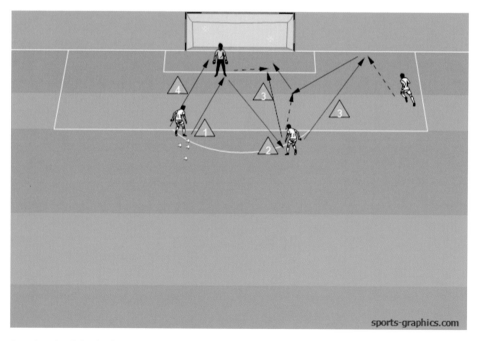

Functional training in the area.

1. Back-pass to goalkeeper, who passes on to second attacker first time.
2. First-time shot or pass to wide attacker.
3. Wide attacker goes to the end line and plays cut-back cross for second attacker to hit.
4. Shot from first attacker.

Colored cone reaction exercise with recovery save.

1. Server calls out side and color (e.g., "Left! Yellow!") and the goalkeeper must move and touch the appropriate cone. The server on that side then shoots.
2. The server chips or throws a ball to the bar and the goalkeeper must recover and save.

Friday: Speed of Action: Reactions and Quickness With Muscle Activation

Although you are primarily using and developing the same energy system on Thursday and Friday (which is the anaerobic-alactic system) the major difference is the volume of work.

Using the exercises shown below, we can account for lower volume on Friday by performing only three sets of three saves with a rest period between each set (appropriate on Friday or day before the match) instead of performing three sets of six saves and then resting

before the next set (more appropriate on Thursday or two days before the match). Both the series of three saves and six saves will work the anaerobic-alactic system, however with sets of only three saves on Friday, the energy system will be engaged but will incur less fatigue due to the shorter bouts of work.

Friday is also the perfect day to work on quick reaction drills to sharpen the goalkeepers reflexes, both physically and menally, before the Saturday game. Exercises like the ones shown below will force the goalkeeper to react very quickly but are of such short duration that it will minimize the liklihood of physical or mental fatigue.

sports-graphics.com

Two-shooter reaction drill. Two shooters approach balls, but only one strikes.

Variations

- Goalkeeper starts facing away from shooters.
- Attackers shoot at far side of goal.

Shooting exercise with heavy cones used to create deflections.

Shooting exercise with extra player used as screen for the goalkeeper.

Goalkeeper reaction exercise with serve from inside post and first-time shot.

Variation

• Serve is tossed to target who punches for goalkeeper to save from seven yards.

WARM-UPS

Warm-ups have evolved significantly over the years. We have come a long way from jogging around the field a few times and sitting in a circle while performing static stretches. To put it simply the overall goal of a warm-up should be to prepare the team and the goalkeepers both physically and mentally to compete at their maximum. Too often the warm-up is seen as something that is done before actual training begins. The team must know that as soon as the warm-up begins, then training begins. Full effort and attention must be paid to all components for it to be a successful warm-up. The two most important benefits from an effective warm-up are a decreased likelihood of injury and improved athletic performance. Often goalkeepers warm up both with the team and also in environments specific to the position. For purposes of this section, the focus is on the general, physical warm-up with the idea that a position-specific warm-up would follow and include many of the exercises in other sections of the book, depending on the session design or game-day preference.

Phases of a Warm-Up

1. **Warming.** The warming phase can be anywhere from 3-10 minutes depending on different variables. An example would be if it is cold outside then you'd want to extend the warming phase to ensure the players' body temperatures are raised. The warming phase can be carried out through jogging, shuffling or skipping or through a technical soccer drill. The main goal is to get each player moving throughout the desired amount of time.

    a. Physical Goals of the Warming Phase

        i.   Increased blood flow

        ii. Increased heart rate

        iii. Increased respiration rate

        iv. Increased body temperature

2.   **Muscular activation and dynamic mobility.** In this phase of the warm-up the players perform dynamic movements that force the body to go through the full range of motion while simultaneously activating muscles through bodyweight movements or against slight resistance (e.g., mini bands). This phase could include anything from balance work and lunging, to squatting. When planning this portion of the warm-up it is important for the coach to understand what demands the day's training session is going to impose upon each player. Their bodies need to be prepared for the intensity and stresses that are ahead.

 a. Examples of activation exercises

  i. Mini-band walking

  ii. Glute bridging

  iii. Front and lateral planks

 b. Examples of dynamic mobility exercises

  i. Inch worms

  ii. Lunge variations (forward, reverse, lateral)

  iii. Squat variations (single leg, two leg, overhead)

  iv. Hip hinge variations

3. **Priming.** This is the most intense stage of the warm-up because the coach needs to fully prepare the team for the activity that will follow. If the coach knows the next activity is a passing drill then obviously he can adjust this part of the warm-up as the passing exercise wouldn't be as intense as, for example, a 1-vs.-1. Similarly, for goalkeepers, a session on explosive diving would feature a more intense warm-up than one where distribution is the main topic.
   a. Examples of priming drills
      i. Plyometric drills
      ii. Short accelerations
      iii. Change of direction drills

Important Reminders for a Successful Warm-Up

1. As stated before, the most important factor in a successful warm-up is ensuring the team understands that full effort and focus is not suggested but required.
2. When planning the warm-up, base the duration, exercises and intensity off what is going to happen in the training session.
3. A great way to get buy-in from the players is to make the warming phase fun. This can be done through soccer drills or fun games that get the players moving. Goalkeepers often benefit from some light competition (e.g., team handball in a club training setting) as part of adding a bit of fun to their warm-up.
4. Keep the players on their toes. Adjust sections of the warm-up on a daily basis so you always keep the players guessing. One of the worst things that can happen in preparing for training is a set routine that the player go through like robots. For goalkeepers, this can mean mixing movement with light handling or pinging a ball, always looking to combine functional elements.

Sample Warm-Ups

1. Warming (5-7 minutes)
   a. Jogging, shuffling and skipping, followed by a simple passing pattern
2. Muscular activation and dynamic mobility (5-7 minutes)
   a. Single-leg glute bridges: 5 on each leg
   b. Lateral plank: 20 seconds on each side
   c. Single-leg squat to quad stretch
   d. Single-leg squat to glute stretch
   e. Inchworms: 5 repetitions
   f. Forward lunges: 5 on each leg
   g. Squats: 5 repetitions
   h. Squats to jump: 5 repetitions
   i. Lateral lunge: 5 on each leg

3. Priming (2-4 minutes)

    a. Quick feet through cones to 15-yard accelerations: 2 each

        i. Forward: 1 foot in each space

        ii. Forward: 2 feet in each space

        iii. Lateral: 2 feet in each space

        iv. Forward shuffle

        v. Backward shuffle

COOL-DOWNS

Similar to warm-ups, cool-downs have changed significantly over time. In years past teams would either leave training directly afterwards or they would do some quick static stretching. Just as with the warm-up, the cool-down needs to be viewed as part of training. It needs to be the beginning of the recovery process for the next day's training session or match. Given the physical toll of training and match play for the goalkeeper, a thoughtful cool-down will similarly allow the keeper to wind down mentally (this is often a good time for the coach to give the goalkeeper feedback) and physically, initiating the recovery process.

REASONS FOR THE COOL-DOWN

1.   Gradually decreases heart rate
2.   Provides opportunity to minimize soreness through stretching and soft-tissue work
3.   Provides opportunity to increase range of motion
4.   Allows team to mentally decompress after tough session or match

SAMPLE COOL-DOWN

As soon as final training exercise or game ends, follow one of the cool-down options.

1. Range-of-motion focus
   a. Once the session ends, the team should lightly jog or walk to a different part of the field to allow their heart rates to lower.

    b.   Working from the feet up, spend 30 seconds on each major muscle group and repeat each muscle group twice.

        i.   Calves, hamstrings, quadriceps, groin and glutes

2.   Quality-of-tissue focus

    a.   Once the session ends the team should lightly jog or walk to a different part of the field to allow their heart rates to lower.

  b. Use a foam roller (or pumped up ball) and gently roll different muscle groups on top of the ball for 30 seconds per muscle group. Repeat twice.

  c. Begin at the feet and have the players work their way up.

    i. Calves, hamstrings, quadriceps, groin and glutes

3. Focus: General

  a. As the players walk, take them through dynamic stretches; hold each stretch for 2 or 3 seconds.

  b. Begin at the feet and have the players work their way up.

    i. Calves, hamstrings, quadriceps, groin and glutes

  c. Be sure to keep moving throughout the entire cool-down.

MOVEMENT AND AGILITY

The ability to cover space in goal and the area, as well as to make rapid, smooth movements to deal with ever-changing circumstances separates top goalkeepers from their peers. Movement and agility training should be core components in any goalkeeper training program, and elements designed to promote and maximize these physical characteristics should be a feature of every goalkeeper training session.

For younger goalkeepers, particularly those less than twelve years old, the focus should be on proper movement (i.e., the technical components of footwork in particular) and on becoming familiar with their ability to use their bodies to block shots. As goalkeepers begin to specialize and mature during their early- to mid-teen years, the emphasis continues to be on clean, crisp movement, but elements of speed and agility, as well as more demanding physical movements can be incorporated as well. The use of increasingly complex exercises, as well as the incorporation of tools such as agility ladders, low hurdles and other props will help the goalkeeper learn to maximize his mobility while sustaining proper technique. It is important to state that all fitness-related work should be designed to aid the goalkeeper's development and sharpen their movement without incurring injury through inappropriate or excessive training.

The following exercises, organized in age groups, represent the progression discussed above, focusing on basic technique for younger players and increasingly complex environments for maturing and senior goalkeepers.

YOUNG GOALKEEPERS

Cone Zig-Zag

Cone zig-zag (1).

Basic footwork cone-to-cone with emphasis on proper movement, balance and form. Encourage young goalkeepers to forego speed at this point and just move cleanly.

Progression

- Work forward through the zig-zag.
- Do footwork around each cone.
- The coach periodically fakes to hit a ball (the goalkeeper must get set).
- To add some extra agility work, dive to cover a ball at each cone.

Cone zig-zag (2).

Add servers who chest-pass the ball to the goalkeeper to save at each cone. Assure that goalkeepers stop and get set at each cone before the shot.

Progression
- Servers roll the ball.
- Servers bounce the ball.
- Servers punt the ball.
- Servers toss a high ball.

FOLLOW-THE-LEADER GOALKEEPER MOVEMENT

Follow-the-leader goalkeeper movement.

One goalkeeper leads for 30 seconds and the other must mimic her movements. Encourage the goalkeepers to emphasize goalkeeper-specific movements (e.g., shuffling, running, back-pedaling, diving, jumping) as well as fun movements (e.g., forward and backward rolls). Change roles and repeat.

Follow-the-leader pairs goalkeeper movement and agility with a ball.

Similar to the previous exercise, the difference is that the player with the ball is the leader and can throw or kick the ball for her partner to save at any time. Encourage frequent exchanges.

MATURING AND SENIOR GOALKEEPERS

Agility Ladder and Save

Agility ladder and save (1).

The goalkeeper takes one step into each rung of the ladder, then proceeds to the cone goal and saves a shot from the server. The emphasis is on clean footwork and speed.

Footwork

* One step per rung of ladder.
* Both feet step into each rung of the ladder.
* One-footed hops (for speed, not height) in each rung.
* Two-footed jumps (for speed, not height) in each rung.
* Carioca.
* Ickey shuffle.

Agility ladder and save (2).

The goalkeeper does footwork through the ladder. The coach periodically throws a ball for the goalkeeper to catch and return. Work in both directions. Use a medicine ball for senior goalkeepers.

Footwork

- Side-step through the ladder, one foot in each rung at a time.
- Starting on the far side of the ladder from the coach, step into and then back out of each rung with both feet.

STICK GOAL MOVEMENT AND SAVE

Stick goal movement and save (1).

The goalkeeper shuffles around a stick (alternate sides) and then saves a shot from the server.

Progression

- Do a push-up, then move around a stick.
- Goalkeeper lies on his back, then gets up and moves around a stick.
- The coach varies types of serve (e.g., punted, drop-kicked, thrown).
- The coach throws a medicine (weighted) ball for the goalkeeper to catch and throw back.

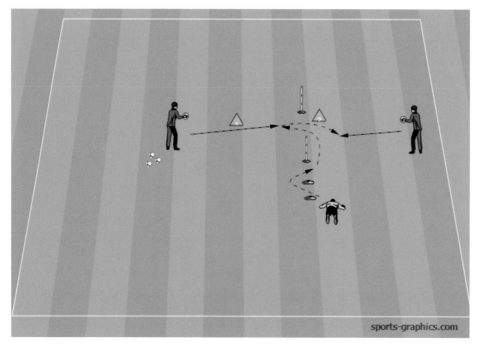

Stick goal movement and save (2).

The goalkeeper lies on his front side, recovers to his feet and does footwork before taking shots from the server on the left (1) and then the server on the right (2). Vary the goalkeeper's starting position and the types of serves.

MOVEMENT WITH LOW HURDLES

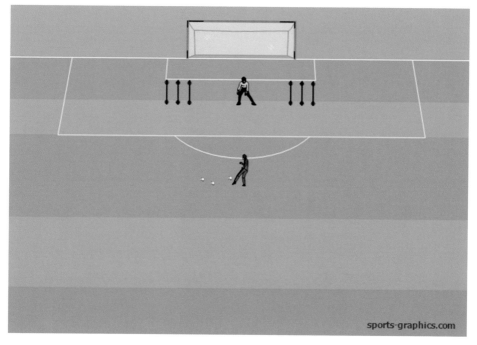

Movement with low hurdles.

The goalkeeper shuffles left or right and works through and back in one set of hurdles (footwork over or around the hurdles) and then saves from the server.

THE CAULDRON

The Cauldron: movement, save and recovery save.

The goalkeeper does footwork over or around the yellow dots along the goal line, then touches the red stick before moving forward to touch the yellow stick. He then dives to stop a low shot to the post from server 1. He then recovers to stop a driven shot from server 2.

Variation

• The goalkeeper recovers after the first save and runs out to touch the ball held by server 2. Server 2 then tosses a ball up near the bar for the goalkeeper to recover and tip or catch.

EXPLOSIVE POWER

Goalkeepers who can use explosive power in their jumping, diving and general shot-stopping will get to balls that cannot otherwise be reached. Therefore, as goalkeepers mature, it is important to cultivate training elements that will allow them to expand their strength and range. These exercises, it must be stressed, are not for use with young (i.e., pre-teen) players and should be added gradually and appropriately for maturing goalkeepers in their early- and mid-teen years. For senior goalkeepers, the most limiting factor for explosive training, as outlined in the periodization section, is the need for recovery before match day.

When designing power-related training, think in terms of the muscle systems used by goalkeepers. Certainly lower-body training is required, enhancing the power of the legs to jump, extension dive and so on; however, core and upper-body training will also aid the lower body in the areas mentioned as well as making the goalkeeper stronger and more injury-resistant in dealing with shots hit with heavy pace, crosses and so on. Thus, a thoughtful, balanced approach is required for training design. The exercises below give examples of power-enhancing exercises specifically tailored to the needs of goalkeepers.

EXPLOSIVE DIVING

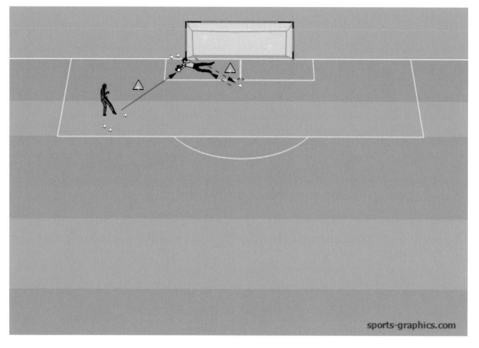

Explosive diving.

The goalkeeper begins on the post with a ball in his hands. He shuffles to the yellow stick and sets the ball down before shuffling and using an extension dive to save the shot from the server. As with all exercises emphasizing power, complete a limited number (e.g., ten) of repetitions total on each side with adequate rest (e.g., 20 seconds) between reps.

CORE CATCHING

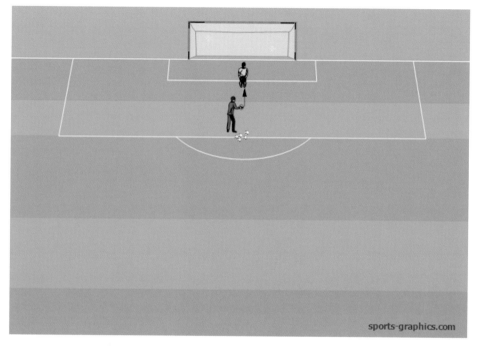

Core catching.

The goalkeeper does sit-ups, making a save from the server each time he recovers to the seated position. The coach can vary his serves from throws to punts to tossing a medicine ball.

POWER EMPHASIS LADDER SEQUENCES

Power emphasis ladder sequences.

The goalkeeper does push-ups or plank work then does high jumps (emphasis on power and control) through the ladder before saving a serve from the coach.

Variations

- Five push-ups; two-footed high jumps through the ladder; save.
- Twenty-second plank (left, right, center); one-footed jumps through the ladder; save.
- Twenty crunches; carry medicine ball through high jumps in ladder; save.

HIGH HURDLE PULL-UP, PUSH-UP SAVES

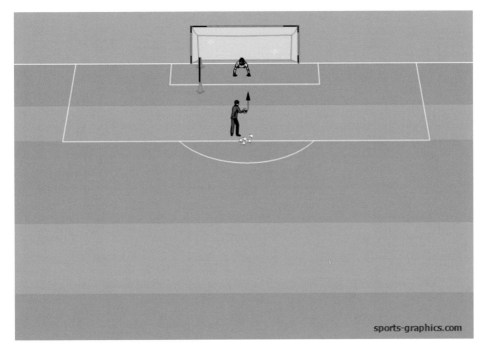

sports-graphics.com

High hurdle pull-up, push-up saves.

The goalkeeper begins in the push-up position and initiates the sequence with a push-up. He then recovers to his feet and jumps up to grab the crossbar (be sure the goal is anchored) and does a pull-up. Finally, he jumps over the high hurdle at his right and jumps back before saving a shot from the server. Repeat five times, and then move the hurdle to the other side for a similar set.

Reactions

Goalkeepers tend to enjoy working through reaction speed exercises and this area of skill is one that becomes more critical as players advance to the higher levels of the game. As the game becomes faster and more complex as players mature, the pace of the shots confronting goalkeepers also dramatically increases.

Therefore, as players enter their teen years, it becomes desirable to include regular exercises designed to increase the speed at which the goalkeeper can react and make decisions. The exercises below are designed to challenge and provide variety for goalkeepers, honing their ability to think and react quickly under pressure.

GOALKEEPER LOOKING AT HIS FEET

Goalkeeper looking at his feet.

The server calls "Shot!" and the goalkeeper must look up quickly and save a volleyed shot.

GOALKEEPER LOOKING AWAY

Goalkeeper looking away.

The goalkeeper faces away from the server. At a command to turn, the goalkeeper must jump around and face the server, who volleys a shot at him to save.

THREE-SHOOTER PROGRESSION

Three-shooter progression.

Use different size balls and hit with pace, testing the goalkeeper's reaction ability.

GOALKEEPER FACING AWAY

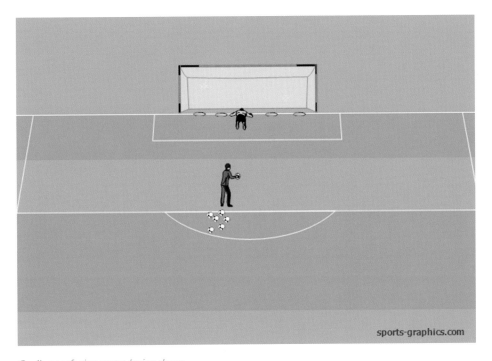

Goalkeeper facing away, laying down.

The server hollers "Go!" and the goalkeeper rises, turns and does footwork over the set of cones indicated by the server. He then works his way back over the cones to the center and stops a shot by the server.

SEATED GOALKEEPER REACTIONS

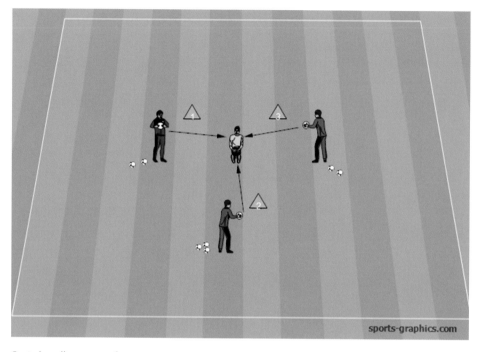

Seated goalkeeper reactions.

The goalkeeper is seated between three servers. The side servers (1 and 3) throw balls for the goalkeeper to push away (one-hand box or open hand), while server 2 volleys balls for the goalkeeper to catch. The sequence is as follows: 1-2-3-2-1 so that servers 1 and 3 are serving after the goalkeeper has saved from server 2. Servers 1 and 3 want to throw just after the goalkeeper has saved from server 2 to force a quick reaction.

STANDING GOALKEEPER REACTIONS

Standing goalkeeper reactions.

This is the same exercise as the previous entry, but now the goalkeeper is standing throughout. Again, the sequence is 1-2-3-2-1, with the side servers trying to play as early as possible after server 2's shot has been saved.

TWO-SHOOTER REACTION DRILL

Two-shooter reaction drill.

Both shooters approach their soccer balls, with one shooting each time.

FUNCTIONAL TRAINING

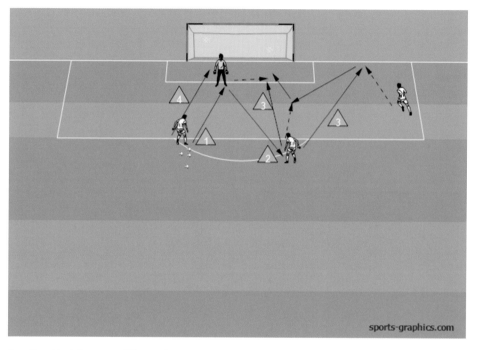

Functional training around the goal.

Server 1 passes to the goalkeeper, who passes to server 2. Server 2 can shoot the first time or push server 3 to the end line, where the latter crosses to server 2 to finish in tight. Then server 1 fires a shot.

DISTRIBUTION REACTIONS

Distribution reactions.

Here the goalkeeper receives serves from the coach and must do one of the following (first time) as commanded by the server. The command must come late (after the ball is served).

1.   Play to target 1.
2.   Play to target 2.
3.   Play to target 3.
4.   Return ball to server first time.
5.   Cover the ball.
6.   Head the ball away (ball bounced high in the D).

TIM MELIA BOX

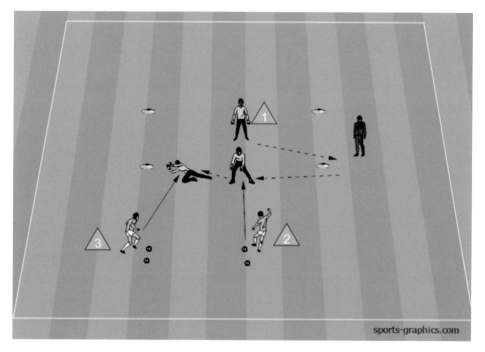

sports-graphics.com

Tim Melia box.

The goalkeeper shuffles around the near-right perimeter cone and then moves to save from the near server 2, before recovering to save from server 3 on a follow-up shot.

NUTRITION

Why include a section on nutrition in a book about goalkeeping? Field players often quip that goalkeepers only run a few yards per match and to many it seems counter-intuitive to worry too much about what a goalkeeper eats. Experience, ironically, indicates that goalkeepers are often among the fittest players on the team, and though their aerobic and anaerobic needs vary from those of field players, their muscular needs, as well as the heavy psychological pressure of playing goalkeeper, require careful nutritional support both for training and match days, as well as recovery periods.

Much attention has been given in high-level coaching circles over the past decade to the notion that proper nutrition is a critical component to maximizing performance. In an era where the game is played faster and by more fit players than ever before, professional coaches employ nutritionists, monitor food intake by their players and even provide pre- and post-game meals designed to prime their athletes for performance and recovery.

If the impact of nutrition is being fully recognized at the professional level, its importance is no less relevant at the youth levels. For young players, the chance to develop good eating habits—in an era when so many American children are overweight and unhealthy— is an important consideration. As children mature, their nutritional needs, particularly as athletes, are often ignored. Student athletes carrying heavy schedules, confronting social stresses, getting limited rest and other impediments to good health and eating are in need of considerable nutritional support for proper maturation and good performance.

The information included here is not meant as a scientific guide to nutrition. Rather, this is an effort to share with parents and coaches general guidelines and specific ideas for helping goalkeepers develop good eating habits and nutritional sufficiency.

In general, athletes must strive to ingest sufficient protein and carbohydrates for the body to burn and recover to improve and sustain performance.

Pre-activity meal. In general, try to eat 2-4 hours before training or matches, focusing on carbohydrates and protein, and avoiding foods that are higher in glycemic value, which do not balance blood glucose levels, leading to greater energy availability. Limit fat intake (Gregg, 1999). Examples of low glycemic index foods include: whole grain pasta, grainy breads, yogurt, nuts, certain fruits (e.g., oranges, grapes, mangos, cherries) and most vegetables.

Between games and on tournament weekends. One of the challenges players face at youth levels is proper eating on tournament weekends. Medium glycemic index foods, such as brown rice, muffins, bran cereals, certain fruits (e.g., strawberries, kiwi, banana watermelon, pineapple) will facilitate recovery and the timely release of energy into the bloodstream for players on tight schedules or facing multiple matches.

Post-activity meal. Finally, it is important to eat a nutritious meal within two hours of working out to help the body replace depleted glycogen stores and make energy available for the next match or training session (ussoccer.com). High glycemic index foods are good choices for these meals, including popcorn, pretzels, some power bars, white pasta, white rice, bagels and so on (Active.com)

HYDRATION

Closely related to nutrition is the need for proper hydration to sustain performance. With the proliferation of energy drinks and continuing popularity of soft drinks, young players are often tempted to consume liquids that will not help them hydrate and that may even hinder their performance.

One of the most astounding lessons of coaching is learning that young people simply do not take in enough water. Many decry the lack of taste or forget to bring along a supply to training or matches. Others just forget to drink enough unless they are told to drink.

Dehydration—the condition of lacking sufficient water—causes a whole series of detrimental characteristics in athletes, from muscle tears and poor heat management to impaired digestion and decreased transport of nutrients and waste products. Indeed, dehydration has been cited as the paramount reason for fading performance (Gregg, 1999).

The simple, widely-held prescription for good hydration is for players to consume at least one-half of their total body weight in ounces of water in a day.

In addition to insufficient hydration through lack of sufficient water consumption, young athletes also tend to start their hydration too close to competition to maximize performance. Indications are that athletes need to plan some 36-72 hours in advance to be fully hydrated. In other words, hydrating to proper levels two days before activity will allow the body to prepare fully for heavy exertion.

On game day, players need to continue to take in water to prepare for and sustain performance. Drinking 12-16 ounces of water in the hours preceding competition is recommended, and

consuming 6-12 ounces for every 20 minutes of competition will help retain performance levels. Players frequently ask how to know how much water they have consumed. An easy reference is to tell them that a large gulp of water is typically similar to an ounce.

Finally, for recovery purposes, players need to drink approximately 20 ounces of water for every pound shed during activity. A simple litmus test is for players to self-monitor urine color. Clear, lemon-colored urine indicates adequate hydration, whereas darker shades of urine (and not needing to urinate) indicate dehydration. Players, including goalkeepers, should be conditioned to continuously monitor and tend to their hydration levels.

Be sure to distinguish among drinks recommended to players. In addition to water, three other types of drinks are available. Those that offer fluid (1) and carbohydrate replenishment (2) are good as well, particularly those balancing sugars and salts to help fluid retention. Avoid energy drinks (3) which often are loaded with caffeine and act as a diuretic, which will speed dehydration (active.com).

REST AND RECOVERY

Just as nutrition and hydration are becoming prevalent points of emphasis with regard to maximizing performance, rest habits of players are being monitored as well. Teams frequently survey players about how well and how much they slept, trying to discover patterns and monitor player health and preparation.

Rest is not a particularly complex topic in the sense that most people would be able to cite the standard recommendation of getting eight hours of sleep as often as possible. Teens, it should be noted, often benefit from and require even more sleep, particularly during periods of heavy exertion and stress.

However, life stressors (e.g., family or work worries) often lead to diminished and lower quality sleep, and prevailing research suggests that poor sleep can quickly and radically reduce performance, whereas quality rest can dramatically improve recovery and performance.

The mental demands on goalkeepers in particular require attention to player rest patterns. Concentration, confidence and consistency—all hallmarks of quality goalkeeping—require goalkeepers to be mentally sharp through every performance, and thus proper rest is a mandatory teaching point of emphasis for coaches and parents.

CHAPTER

03

CHAPTER 3

DECISION MAKING: TACTICAL SITUATIONS

BACK-PASSES AND BUILD-UP PLAY WITH THE FEET

The evolution of the game over the past 25 years has seen the goalkeeper's role as a pressure-release and a central figure in the build-up dramatically change. Prior to 1992 and the change of the back-pass rule (which had allowed the goalkeeper to pick up the ball on any pass back from his own players), the goalkeeper was a fairly conservative figure who killed play at most opportunities by grabbing the ball and either throwing or punting, often over distance.

The past decade in particular has seen the emergence of tactics that demand the goalkeeper be an outstanding technical player who can receive and play a wide array of passes, often under pressure from an opponent. Pep Guardiola's Barcelona in particular welcomed the opposition to press their team up high, relying on the goalkeeper to help break pressure with his feet. Manuel Neuer of Bayern Munich and World Cup champion Germany, arguably the best goalkeeper in the world at the time of this writing, is a virtual sweeper-keeper, often ranging well beyond his area either to cut out service behind a high back line or in an effort to provide close support to his team in possession.

If the demands upon the goalkeeper's ability to play with his feet have increased, how does that impact the training of goalkeepers at every level? Clearly, much attention must be paid to the technical demands of dealing with back-passes and participating in the build-up. Indeed, top goalkeepers are now among the most technically gifted players with their feet on the team. However, the tactical elements involved in each of these situations must also be discussed and trained with the goalkeeper and the team so that there is seamless understanding of how to cope with each situation on game day.

BACK-PASSES

Back-passes: Goalkeepers training to receive and pass the ball.

- Coordination between the entire back line and the goalkeeper must be rehearsed, as a back pass could originate from any back-line—or midfield—player.
- When is a back-pass to the goalkeeper called for? When the options for the teammate in possession become limited from pressure by an opponent. Cues for the goalkeeper include a teammate pressured and facing his own goal, and situations where the team is in tight space in the back or middle third and numbers-even or numbers-down near the ball.
- Ideally, the goalkeeper initiates the sequence by calling for the ball.
- Even before the ball is played toward the goalkeeper, he must begin to read the situation. Can the back-pass be completed safely? How many opponents are in a

position to pressure the ball? What are the best options when the ball is received?

- Particularly at the youth level, the goalkeeper is encouraged to move beyond the width of the goal (outside the post) and to the near side where play permits to receive. This is a form of safeguard against either a miss-hit pass at the goal or a pressure situation where the goalkeeper could be confronted before goal by an onrushing attacker.

- As the ball travels, continue to assess the situation. Will an opponent be able to pressure the ball or, worse, arrive with the goalkeeper? Can the goalkeeper play with multiple touches or must he clear immediately? Which foot will be used and how can the goalkeeper play away from pressure? It is critical that the goalkeeper move to the ball if he will be pressured and play as early as possible.

- Again, while the ball travels, the goalkeeper makes a final decision as to his target for distribution. Long? Short? Can the target player turn or will he be pressured (as this will affect whether the ball is played off the front or back foot)?

- Once the ball is received, if there is no pressure, the goalkeeper can take a moment to assess the options. If playing with a lead or if the team has been under pressure, he may want to slow the game a bit. On the contrary, if his team trails or the other team is poorly situated to defend in some areas, he may want to play quickly.

- Finally, once the ball is played, the goalkeeper must continue to provide communication to the target. Can he turn? How many opponents are moving to pressure? What would be that player's best option?

- The goalkeeper must be prepared to either remain in position to support the attack or drop to his box and goal if the ball is lost.

Again, the most important factor in back-passes is coordination. Goalkeepers and back-line players benefit enormously from a few minutes here and there to knock the ball around, simulating back-passes and distribution. The coach must also make clear his or her preferences regarding the goalkeeper's distribution (e.g., long, short, hand, foot, to specific targets) as part of dictating the team's philosophy in possession.

BUILD-UP PLAY

Similar to and related to the tactical topic of back-passes is the subject of build-up play with the feet. Whereas the back-pass topic focuses on the execution of a pass to the goalkeeper and the subsequent options of the goalkeeper in possession, for build-up play the specific emphasis is upon the role of the goalkeeper in the team's transition from the back third. Certainly the topics overlap, but the tactical cues for build-up play emphasize the goalkeeper's choices in possession.

- In every case, the assumption here is that the goalkeeper has the time to execute different choices in distribution and therefore must select the proper pass.
- Critically, the coach must work with the team and goalkeeper to lay out the tactical preferences in every situation.

1. From a goal kick, what are the preferences? Should he play short to an outside back if that player is open? Does the coach want to play the strikers directly to start the attack?

2. In a punting situation, should the goalkeeper release the ball immediately and as far as possible, or is a throw or short kick to back or midfielder preferred?

3. When playing in the flow of play, what are the team's tactical preferences for the goalkeeper? Is the goal to draw the opposing team forward, stretching their lines and facilitating indirect build-up? Or is the goal to play out the opposition's forward and midfield lines with direct play?

4. How much do game situation (e.g., early, late, ahead, behind), weather and the nature of the opposition influence the team's priorities and therefore the goalkeeper's choices?

5. When playing from a back-pass, as discussed above, what are the distribution priorities for the goalkeeper?

The abilities and proclivities of the goalkeeper and the team will heavily influence the tactical planning of the coach with regard to the goalkeeper's role in the build-up. If the goalkeeper is mobile, sharp with his feet and confident playing under the defense, he can be deployed higher behind the defense and play a more active role in the build-up. If, however, he tends to play closer to his line and focus on shot-stopping, the goalkeeper can have a more limited role in the build-up phase.

THROUGH-BALLS

Dealing with through-balls is one of the most challenging tactical situations that goalkeepers confront. As with the closely related topics of clearances and build-up play, a whole range of factors influence the goalkeeper's approach to cutting out through-balls played by the opposition. The coach must work closely with the goalkeepers and the back line to discuss the role of each player in defending the space behind the back line. Here are some tactical considerations for the goalkeeper.

- The starting point for the discussion between the goalkeeper and the coach is the goalkeeper's ability and comfort level in playing off of his line and under the defense. Highly mobile, technically sharp and confident goalkeepers can often be deployed much higher than stay-at-home types, allowing the team to shrink the space between the back line and the goalkeeper.
- Similarly, what are the characteristics of the back-line players? Do they run well and make good decisions, allowing for a more aggressive, higher defense? Or are they a more passive, drop-oriented group that wants to keep play in front of them?
- What are the coaches' preferences? Some coaches base their defending on pressure, and want the whole team aggressively hunting the ball (high line and active goalkeeper). Others believe absorbing pressure and conservative defending will allow the team to be more competitive and they may want the back line and goalkeeper staying home.
- Game conditions also influence the approach here. The team will likely play more aggressively in some situations (e.g., down a goal late) than others (e.g., up a goal late). Weather can influence the defending approach, with wet fields and wind perhaps shaping the tactical philosophy in a given game. Finally, the opponent is a crucial consideration. Teams that possess fast, attacking personalities that try to get in behind the back line will require a different approach than those that use less mobile targets and attack in an indirect fashion.
- Communication between the back-line players and the goalkeeper when a through-ball is played will be a decisive factor in the team's success at defending critical space. The goalkeeper has the best view of every through-ball situation, given that

he is moving forward while any of his back-line players are running toward their own goal. Thus, the goalkeeper must become adept at making a decisive, accurate call as to whether he will be coming after a through-ball or remaining near his line.

- Starting position is another important consideration. Adopting a higher line gets one closer to the backs and the ball, but also exposes the space in behind the goalkeeper and he may be chipped. Conversely, starting closer to the line reduces the possibility of being chipped, but the goalkeeper then has more ground to cover and the space behind the back line is greater.

- If the goalkeeper opts to remain near his line, he must guide the back-line players to deal with the through-ball. Whether the goalkeeper calls for a back-pass or a clearance to cut out the threat, he must both move to the appropriate position and also provide feedback to the defenders until the danger is ended.

- If the goalkeeper opts to deal with the through-ball by going to the ball, he must make the verbal call and close the space, all the while being ready to change his call to a clearance if he will arrive late and the defender should thus press on, prepared to clear the ball if the goalkeeper cannot get to the ball. Note that the defender may also decide to clear the ball on his own if he determines the pressure is too great from an on-rushing attacker or the goalkeeper's run will get him there after the attacker.

- Another important consideration is where the goalkeeper will reach the ball. If the goalkeeper will get to the ball outside of the 18-yard box, he will have to use his feet or head to clear the ball. Clearances must travel high, wide and far, avoiding any on-rushing attacker in particular. If the goalkeeper will reach the ball inside his box, he must decide whether he will be able to receive the ball while standing or if he will need to leave his feet and take the ball under pressure from an oncoming opponent.
- Anytime the goalkeeper will take the ball, one or more defenders must shield the goalkeeper from the onrushing attacker, keeping themselves between the attacker and the ball until the goalkeeper has made the save or clearance. Additionally, a defender must run past the goalkeeper, getting into position between the goalkeeper and the goal, ready to clear any rebound.
- Finally, after the ball is brought under control by a defender or the goalkeeper, or the ball is cleared, there is still danger for the back line and the goalkeeper. The goalkeeper must distribute or recover and the back line must transition, either to defending a throw after a clearance over the touch-line, or to an attacking posture. All of this movement must be completed in concert so that if danger erupts again, the group is ready to respond.

1-VS.-1 SITUATIONS

The goalkeeper faces few more complex and challenging situations than a 1-vs.-1 confrontation with an attacker. Though any situation where an attacker is in against a goalkeeper is a 1-vs.-1 situation, for purposes of this tactical discussion, the focus will be on breakaways. Other 1-vs.-1 situations, including a loose ball scramble before goal where the attacker gets in alone, or settles a cross, will be dealt with in the relevant areas of the text. Breakaways, then, are a difficult conundrum for the goalkeeper, who defends a 24 × 8 goal alone against an attacker who can shoot, chip, dribble, change speeds and angles and even potentially recover a rebound and score. The goalkeeper, then, needs to be prepared for any of these eventualities and also, very importantly, must try to eliminate as many choices as possible so that he has the opportunity to make a save. The preparation for the goalkeeper to deal with breakaways involves technical, tactical and psychological training, and a measured approach from the coach, who should work with the goalkeeper on these situations in short stints. Training breakaways for brief, intense periods limits the toll on the goalkeeper, physically and mentally, and also creates realistic training pressure. Here are tactical cues to help goalkeepers and coaches break down and solve breakaway situations.

PART I: RECOGNITION AND CLOSING

- As with any save situation, starting position is an important consideration. A breakaway will become apparent to the goalkeeper when the attacker gets in behind the defense. The goalkeeper's starting position may vary depending on what he had anticipated (higher if he was hoping to cut out a through-ball, for instance), but generally speaking, the goalkeeper will be near the top of his 6-yard box when he recognizes that a breakaway is emerging.

- "Should I go?" If the attacker is shoulder-ahead of the last defender, the goalkeeper must begin to close as the attacker gets within 5 yards of the 18-yard box. If, however, a defender still has a chance to make the play, the goalkeeper should wait as long as possible (i.e., until the ball crosses the 18-yard box line) before joining. Always give the defender every chance to deal with the situation.

- *Closing.* As the goalkeeper recognizes the breakaway, his first priority is to close the space with the attacker while also making sure the latter cannot chip the ball over the on-rushing goalkeeper. Critical cues in this regard include the amount of pressure on the shooter, as a sprinting dribbler fighting off a defender is unlikely to be able to pull up and chip over a goalkeeper. Also, the goalkeeper should use the time when the ball is out of the attacker's feet to close, as no shot is possible unless the attacker is in contact with the ball. As the attacker comes within 20-22 yards of goal, the goalkeeper should begin to close from his starting position. Closing involves a few long strides to cover ground quickly, and then short, choppy steps as the goalkeeper gets closer, allowing the goalkeeper to make adjustments or set his feet. Throughout, the goalkeeper uses a big posture with the hands out wide and chest up, presenting a large, intimidating target for the attacker.

Shot! The goalkeeper takes a set-step in close, prepared to save.

- Shot! During the closing phase, the goalkeeper must be vigilant, watching for cues that the attacker is about to shoot. If the attacker is about to shoot, the goalkeeper must set his feet, returning to his ready position, as no lateral movement is possible while striding forward. Cues that an attacker will shoot include a longer touch; looking up, then down; and a longer back-swing of the striking foot.

PART II: TAKING CONTROL

- As the goalkeeper closes with the attacker, he begins to limit the latter's options. For the goalkeeper, the emphasis is on trying to get control of the situation and force the attacker to choose an option that is less likely to produce a goal (e.g., shooting from a bad angle, dribbling to within distance of a blocking goalkeeper).
- The goalkeeper should attempt to read the touches of the attacker, looking for a moment to take the ball away while the ball is out of the attacker's feet. In other words, when the attacker takes a touch, the goalkeeper should look to dive into the path of the ball. Better attackers and those with little pressure will take shorter, more controlling touches, making it more difficult for the goalkeeper to find his touch. Note that once the goalkeeper has closed the distance with the attacker, any touch to either side and forward (which is an attempt to change the angle) should

be cut out by an aggressive blocking dive by the goalkeeper. Allowing this touch will give the attacker an opportunity to open up the goal and perhaps push past the goalkeeper.

- Speak up! The goalkeeper should call for the ball in a breakaway situation. The call should be loud and decisive, trying to upset the attacker's thinking.
- Be unpredictable. Again, the control in this situation rests with the attacker at the start. Faking even slightly while there has not been a moment to take the ball, changing one's footwork or any other visual trick to make it difficult for the attacker to read the goalkeeper should be used to alter the balance of control.
- Use the angle to the goalkeeper's advantage. Breakaways from wider angles present opportunities for the goalkeeper to limit the attacker's options. Attackers are taught to play to the back side and low on the goalkeeper. Knowing this, advanced goalkeepers become proficient at showing slightly more of the goal on the near side, tempting the attacker to work into the smaller portion of the goal. If the goalkeeper can close the attacker and then force a touch to the near post, his job has become considerably easier, as he now has a much smaller goal to defend and the attacker's touch often creates an opportunity for the goalkeeper to seize the ball. The other subtle element in the goalkeeper's favor in this situation is the fact that attackers generally try to avoid the goalkeeper's feet when the latter commit. The reason for this is that the attacker would rather deal with the head and hands of the goalkeeper than his cleats. Thus, when the goalkeeper commits to the near post, his feet will be to the back post, and the attacker may oblige his wishes by bringing the ball to the near post.

PART III: WINNING THE DUEL

- Once the goalkeeper has closed with the attacker, he must win the duel.
- Approach angle. Young goalkeepers often get to the point where they are ready to take the ball away, and find that they have come straight on to the attacker and cannot figure out which side to dive and block on. The result is often a frozen goalkeeper who either leads with their feet or hopes the attacker will shoot. A fix for this concern for young goalkeepers is to approach, particularly the last few yards, from an angle slightly off of straight at the ball, creating an easier decision as to

which diving blocking side to use. Note that this does not mean a curved run that opens up the goal, but a very subtle adjustment in the final steps. Conversely, more experienced goalkeepers will generally come straight on to the attacker, creating a more intimidating presence and forcing the attacker to make a decision perhaps before they are ready.

- When to take the ball. If the attacker has not shot and the goalkeeper has not found a moment to take the ball when it is out of the attacker's feet, the goalkeeper can force the issue if he has closed well. Teach the goalkeeper to get into the attacker's feet in this situation. In other words, if the attacker is keeping the ball tight, he is likely going to try to dribble the goalkeeper and his other options will be extremely limited. Therefore, the goalkeeper must become accustomed to grasping control by getting into the attacker's feet to take the ball. Seizing the ball and separating the attacker from it wins the duel for the goalkeeper.

- The crucial moment in this context is the decision to take the ball. What if the attacker suddenly decides to shoot or push the ball beyond the goalkeeper? These are the toughest challenges for the goalkeeper. He must stay big, and on his feet until he is very close to the ball. Goalkeepers who drop or stop instead of going after the ball are often beaten at the last second because they fail to stay big until the last second before the save. Get tight and then get into the attacker's feet.

DEALING WITH CROSSES

As goalkeepers mature, defending crosses becomes an integral part of the tactical demands of the game. Teams develop the ability to serve balls into all spaces before goal, and attackers become more adept at disguising runs and finishing, complicating the picture and challenging the goalkeeper's ability to control the area and handle tough shots from in close. It is therefore mandatory that goalkeepers become comfortable with commanding the defense, setting their own angles, focusing their depth perception, taking the ball under pressure and making a variety of saves in their area in crossing situations.

• *Recognition.* As with other tactical situations for the goalkeeper, the first cue for dealing with crosses is recognition that a cross may be imminent. The goalkeeper must get to the proper starting position (see below), and also take a read on the tactical situation. How many defenders will be available before goal to help deal with the cross? How many attackers are present? Where are they? How far from goal are they? The goalkeeper must get a good look at the situation and then communicate what he sees to his back-line players, concerning marking assignments in particular.

Dealing with a wide cross: Starting position.

- *Starting position.* This is one of the toughest elements of the game for younger goalkeepers to learn. In general, the goalkeeper must always protect the near post if a shot is possible, while understanding that the back post represents the most difficult point for him to defend (it's easier to move forward than backward in pursuit of the ball). The tendency is to overplay the near post or to drift to the near post as the play develops. Every goalkeeper will need to find their own starting position depending on their own characteristics and confidence. As a guide, wider ball positions allow for the goalkeeper to start further from the near post, as a direct shot becomes unlikely. As the ball position becomes more central, the goalkeeper is drawn to his near post to protect against a direct shot to that area.

Crosses from narrow positions require the goalkeeper to defend her near post.

- *Second goal consideration on close crosses.* If the attacker threatening to cross drives the end line and dribbles toward goal the goalkeeper must close on and possibly past his near post, depending on the penetration of the attacker to deal with the threat. This is necessary to prevent a near-post goal. However, as the goalkeeper closes on his near post, the remainder of the goal opens behind him. It is useful, therefore, to think in terms of a second goal, stretching from the near post straight to the top of the 6-yard box. The goalkeeper must defend the primary goal throughout, and particularly that near post, but if he can also cut out passes through that second goal, he will increase his effectiveness and help his back line deal effectively with short crosses.

The goalkeeper cuts out crosses from the near-post position.

- *Distance from the line.* Younger goalkeepers generally start from near or on their line in dealing with crosses. As goalkeepers mature and attempt to expand their range, they tend to adopt a somewhat higher (2-3 yards) starting position on wide crosses, allowing them greater ability to control their area.

- *Open stance.* The goalkeeper should adopt an open stance to the ball before the serve. This is to say that he should not face directly toward the ball, but should pull the up-field foot back to orient himself partially up-field. This orientation allows the goalkeeper to be focused on the ball and the evolving tactical situation, and also saves time as the goalkeeper moves to deal with the cross.

- *Another look.* Goalkeepers should learn to recognize the touch before a cross from an attacker. This touch is typically longer, setting up the footwork to cross. After this touch, the goalkeeper should get one more look at the evolving tactical situation. Where are the runners and defenders? Where is the greatest danger? From the ball position and run of the attacker, where is the ball most likely to be served? Communicate!

- *The decision.* To go or not to go, that is the question. Younger goalkeepers tend to be very inconsistent in assessing whether they can go retrieve a cross, which makes

sense as they develop their ability to read the ball in the air and also their own physical skills. A good rule of thumb for young goalkeepers is to ask them to deal with balls served into the 6-yard box and between the posts. This frame of reference simplifies the responsibilities of the goalkeeper and makes the roles of the defenders easier to define as well.

- *Make the call.* If the goalkeeper decides to take the ball, he must call "Keeper!" If he cannot get to the ball, he must call "Away!" As goalkeepers mature and refine their ability to read crosses, they must make the call ever earlier.

- *Taking the ball.* Goalkeepers become adept at reading the height and trajectory of the serve, and at selecting the right angle of approach to the ball. The goalkeeper must learn to take the ball as early as possible, limiting the possibility that an attacker can get on the end of the serve. One of the critical skills in dealing with high serves across the goal is driving through the jump for the ball with the up-field knee pushing through the save. Other considerations include whether to punch or tip the ball (in traffic or difficult conditions), remembering to punch the ball back from the direction it came or punch or tip the ball in the direction it is traveling if it is contacted in the back half of the goal area.

- *Finish the save.* One of the most common errors among young goalkeepers is the tendency to drop the ball after catching a cross. It is important for the goalkeeper to high-point the ball (catch it at the highest possible point) and then hold the ball high as one sets one's feet, keeping it away from attackers and also demonstrating control to the referee should there be a collision.

- If the call is "Away!" the goalkeeper must move with the ball and get set to deal with any knock-down or shot. Marshalling the defense to mark, pressure, block shots and clear rebounds is an essential part of the goalkeeper's role in defending crosses.

DEFENDING CORNER KICKS

Defending corner kicks is a team responsibility with special emphasis upon the goalkeeper. Youth goalkeepers in particular find defending corner kicks very challenging because opponents can flood the area and serve the ball into the crowd. As goalkeepers mature, they must learn to organize their defense, deal with being marked by an opponent, make good decisions regarding whether to go after the ball and clear the area.

- Prevent corner kicks through good defending. Many corner kicks can be avoided entirely through intelligent defending (e.g., defend the end line) and coordination between the goalkeeper and the back line. Coaches should emphasize to goalkeepers that controlling the ball in save situations can prevent many corners as well.

- *Organization.* Every team has a philosophy and set-up for defending corner kicks, typically a blend of man-to-man and zonal marking. The goalkeeper must be the coach on the field in these situations, knowing what the coach wants for defending posture and cajoling teammates to get to defending positions early and sort out marking assignments where relevant. The goalkeeper has the best view of the situation and must be a vocal, firm presence.

- Man-to-man or zonal marking? The pendulum between these two forms of marking swings back and forth in the tactical game. At the time of this writing, a blend of the two philosophies prevails, with most senior youth teams deploying players at both posts to support the goalkeeper, a zonal arrangement in the 6-yard box, and a few players man-marking what are deemed to be the most dangerous opponents. The goalkeeper must know the responsibilities of all of the positions and players and assure that everyone is where they should be.

- *Short corners.* Many teams will use a short corner kick play on occasion, running two players to the ball. The goalkeeper must know how the coach wants to deal with this and any other trick play situations. Most teams send a second defender to the corner and attack the ball as soon as it is put in play.

Goalkeeper marked on a corner-kick situation.

- *Dealing with a player marking the goalkeeper.* Often, attacking teams will place one or more players in front of the goalkeeper in preparation for a corner kick. This is a legal practice, as long as the players do not impede the goalkeeper's ability to move to the ball. There is considerable gray area here. Attackers learn to move to the ball—slowly—right along the path the goalkeeper needs to use. How should a goalkeeper deal with this situation? First, alert the referee to the player's presence, pointing out that the player cannot impede your movement to the ball. Most goalkeepers then seek the help of the center backs, asking them to bump and screen the attacker so that the goalkeeper can get to the ball.

- *Read and decide.* When the ball is served, the goalkeeper has only a brief moment to decide whether to go get the ball (call "Keeper!") or ask the team to clear the ball (call "Away!"). Factors beyond the flight and likely point of arrival of the ball include the ability to get to the ball (is there a path to the ball?), weather (it is tougher to get to and corral the ball on a very wet field), game situation, and opponent (one may be more eager for help from the team to clear against a very tall, aggressive team).

- *Clear the area.* When the ball leaves the 18-yard box, the goalkeeper should release the players on the posts and push the team out of the area. This action creates an offside space where the goalkeeper can deal with any recycled effort by the opponent to play the ball back into the area.

DEFENDING FREE KICKS

Free-kick situations require precision coordination between the goalkeeper and field players. Unmarked players, poorly-built walls and miscommunication all lead to goals that the team can prevent with proper preparation. For his part, the goalkeeper must again be the coach on the field, organizing and demanding performance from his teammates. Free kicks are especially challenging in the sense that every instance is different: Direct or indirect? How many players in the wall? Shot, serve or passing sequence? What are the special abilities of the players on the ball? All of these questions must be answered very quickly and decisively to defend free kicks in a successful manner. The goalkeeper must understand the philosophy and prerogatives of the coach regarding defending free kicks, work with the other field players cleanly and quickly implement the necessary steps to avoid conceding in free-kick situations.

- *Variables.* Free kicks present many variables that influence the defending choices by the goalkeeper and team. For example, a direct free kick 90 yards from goal does not require a great deal of organization from the goalkeeper (perhaps other than helping set the height of the back line), whereas an indirect free kick from 6 yards before goal requires the goalkeeper to mobilize the entire team on his line in a desperate effort to keep the ball out of the goal.

  1. *Distance.* Below is a chart displaying generalizations about the number of players used in the defending wall. These numbers will vary with age and ability level of the players. Shots or serves from distance also require the goalkeeper to work with the back line to set an offside or restraining line. This line is critical in the sense that raising it gives the goalkeeper more room to deal with the serve, but also expands the area that has to be covered after the ball is hit by the goalkeeper and the retreating defenders.

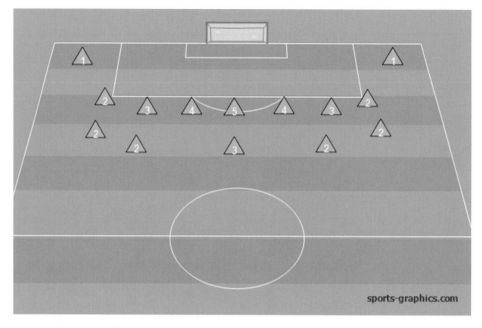

Suggested free-kick wall numbers by distance and angle.

2. *Angle.* Wide angle balls more often than not lead to service near the goal rather than a shot and thus require different preparation (smaller wall and more players marking).

3. Direct or indirect? This is especially crucial in situations where a direct shot is possible. If the team deploys a bullet (i.e., a player who runs at the ball after the first touch in an indirect-kick situation), that player must be known to the goalkeeper and be placed where he does not impede the goalkeeper's view of the ball.

• Once the location and the nature of the kick are established, the team must quickly execute the following steps, with the goalkeeper in control and ready for an unexpected set play by the opponent.

1. Front the ball. It is now common practice to have a player stand a few yards from the ball to prevent the kick being taken quickly and to allow the team time to set up its defensive stance. It is of vital importance that the goalkeeper be immediately concerned with the possibility of a fast restart until the official

steps in and halts play. Then the goalkeeper can go about placing the wall, checking marking assignments and finding his own starting position.

2. Build the wall. Determine the number of players, if any, to be placed in the wall. Some teams have an attacker adjust the position of the wall, but most have the goalkeeper move to her post and direct the wall into position. The goalkeeper should use both visual (e.g., pointing) and verbal instructions to move the wall. At the youth level, placing one player's body beyond the line of the post is recommended to protect against a bent hit around the wall and into the goal. Typically, one player in the wall faces the goalkeeper and moves with her directions. Note also that the wall is usually built about 7 yards from the ball and when the referee moves the wall back, the goalkeeper will need to reset the proper position for the wall.

The goalkeeper on the post, setting a wall to defend a free kick.

3. Get to the proper position to save. The wall is built to defend the near post. The goalkeeper therefore has primary responsibility for the back post. She should therefore adopt a starting position off the shoulder of the last defender on the

central side of the wall. This way, she still has a chance to cover behind the wall, but is situated to see the ball and get to the back side of the goal as well.

4.   Survey the marking of the other field players. Are the opponents marked by the degree of danger they pose? In most cases, mark the players closest to the goal first. In situations where a serve is likely (e.g., wide angle, distance and indirect kicks), it is useful to mark tall or high-scoring players regardless of their starting position. Make any adjustments quickly and decisively.

5.   When the official blows her whistle to restart play, the goalkeeper's focus must be entirely on defending the shot or serve.

6.   Once the danger has passed, the goalkeeper should encourage her teammates to push out of the back third and avoid creating similar free-kick situations.

DEFENDING PENALTY KICKS

This is the ultimate challenge for a goalkeeper. Whether a penalty is called by an official during the match or the team enters a penalty kick shootout to determine an outcome, considerable pressure is placed on the goalkeeper to try to defend her goal against long odds. The large size of the full-sized goal, at 8 × 24 , and the short distance of the shot (36), make the goalkeeper's task a daunting one. What's more, players at higher levels consistently train to finish penalties, and the opposing coach will send their most accomplished finishers to the line. Thus, the message to goalkeepers in general is one of understanding that the odds are stacked against their position in this situation. Players will score on penalty kicks. In his outstanding book on the subject (*Twelve Yards: The Art and Psychology of the Perfect Penalty Kick,* Penguin, 2014), Ben Lyttleton cited a study of the 2009/2010 Series A season (page 149) that noted that 74% of penalties that season were converted. What must also be noted, however, is that some goalkeepers excel in penalty-kick situations, while others seem lost. So what, then, are the best coaching points for coaching goalkeepers to defend penalties?

The goalkeeper making herself big before a penalty is taken.

The goalkeeper ready to defend a penalty kick.

- Understand that much of taking and stopping penalties is mental. The kicker has a set of habits that help her succeed and so does the goalkeeper. The best advice in this regard is to establish and maintain a set of success-breeding habits as a goalkeeper while disrupting those of the shooter. Sometimes these two strands overlap. Some goalkeepers wait to enter the goal until the last moment, while others tap both posts, hang from the bar or stand there trying to look big. Others try to approach the shooter, offering good luck wishes or questioning some minor point with the official to delay the shooter.

- Should I guess? The answer is an emphatic "No!" Studies have amply demonstrated that guessing does not lead to a healthier save percentage. According to Lyttleton's book (page 149), 51% of shooters will place the ball to the goalkeeper's right; 39% to his left, and 10% down the middle. Some goalkeepers become adept at reading the footwork of the shooter (e.g., it's very difficult to shoot the ball opposite of the pointing direction of the shooter's plant foot). This is a late cue, but can be very helpful for senior goalkeepers who are comfortable trying to read that last step.

- Other tips. Some goalkeepers find it useful to feint to one side during the attacker's run-up, trying to force a late change of plan for the shooter. Quick, aggressive goalkeepers sometimes take a quick step off of their line and then react, hoping to cut the angle before the shot is hit. While this is technically not legal, it is rarely called and at worst leads to a re-kick, which can be a dicey mental proposition for the shooter (e.g., "Do I go back to the same spot or change my plan?")

Every goalkeeper finds a pattern for dealing with penalty kicks that helps them cope with this specialized situation, and tactics that help some will hinder others. It's crucial that the coach encourage the goalkeeper to be resilient when scored upon. Indeed, goalkeepers who can save just one or two efforts in a shootout usually give their team a chance to win the match.

CHAPTER

04

CHAPTER 4

GOALKEEPING INSIDE-OUT: PSYCHOLOGICAL PREPARATION

"Catch them being good!" This quote (and book title) attributed to innovative World Cup champion coach Tony DiCicco couldn't be more true, especially when applying it to molding and managing young goalkeeping talent in a training and playing environment.

No position in soccer requires more concentration, more focus or more resilience than the goalkeeping position. That is why it has been in the forefront of having position-specific training. However, not all teams have the luxury of employing their own goalkeeper coach. Therefore, it's crucial for all coaches (not just goalkeeper coaches) to have some understanding of how to create a team and training environment that's conducive to building high levels of confidence and mental toughness in their goalkeepers. In addition to creating this environment, the coach is responsible for motivating the goalkeepers and helping them overcome setbacks and disappointments that occur with more dire consequences than they do with outfield players. The equation that coaches need to remember regarding the psychological development of their goalkeeper is: COMFORT + COMPETENCE = CONFIDENCE!

The pathway of an elite player is marked by several critical points that require psychological adaptation in order to continue progression. —Gloria Balogue, sports psychologist

COMFORT IS ABOUT BUILDING TRUST AND RESILIENCE

Before a goalkeeper can be confident in his ability he must be competent in his core skills. To become more competent in his skill set he must first trust and respect the coach enough to let down his guard and take in the information the coach is trying to give him to improve his game. Therefore, the first step in building the goalkeeper's confidence is to build a trusting, supportive and challenging environment with the goalkeeper that leads to a relationship built on psychological safety.

These softer skills of coaching include man-management, emotional and psychological support, creating a competitive and challenging training culture, dealing with public expectations (parents at the youth level) and the ability to divert pressure away from his goalkeeper, and are crucial because his mistakes can often be more glaring when compared to field players. The best coaches make the players feel comfortable with pressure and are comfortable with it themselves. They should have the ability to empower players to take risks and deal with mistakes convincing them that this is where the most learning takes place. Coaches should consistently strive to facilitate a mindset that is conducive to optimal performance.

Coaches need to establish a rapport with their goalkeeper by communicating often with them on both the positive and negative actions they have performed in training and games. Different people react differently to various approaches. It will take some effort on the part of the coach to figure out what works best with each of his goalkeepers. Over time the coach, by observing closely, will have a good idea of what kind of approach they respond best to. Some goalkeepers will know exactly when they have made a mistake and there will be no need to point it out. For others, the coach may have to ride them pretty hard to get the best out of them. Then there are some that will constantly need positive reinforcement based on their personality. If you don't know and understand your players, then how can you effectively coach and develop them? It's the coach's job to know what type of feedback works best for them and provide it to them.

CREATING THE CORRECT MINDSET: A CHALLENGING AND SUPPORTIVE ENVIRONMENT

Research has confirmed "the importance and significance of the role of coaches through the creation of challenging situations in practice, fostering high expectations, providing support as well as serving as role models" (Connaughton, Wadey et al., 2008: Thelwell et al., 2010). By encouraging a trusting relationship and focusing on the positives, we certainly are not advocating being soft on your players—helping them through every struggle and not letting them sometimes stumble over the little things—as this will only prevent them from developing coping skills, mastery and, in the end, the true confidence to overcome obstacles. Giving goalkeepers the chance to recognize that you are there for them, even when you're not commanding their every move—making them capable of picking themselves up when they fail—is the only way they will internalize the strength of the coaching bond and a sense of their own competence. There is a tendency for coaches today to ignore a player's requirements to develop individually and to recognize that nature, along with the correct amount of nurturing, is an essential ingredient to reaching their potential. Constantly stepping in to protect maturing young players—or assuming they always need you to protect them—may hurt them more than help them in the long run. This compulsion to intervene and make them feel comfortable must be tempered with the need to help them build resiliency and grit. They must be gradually exposed to, rather than shielded from, demanding situations in training and games in order to learn how to cope.

Instead the goalkeepers should be challenged regularly. In addition to being stretched physically, training should also incorporate some form of psychological pressure. This could include environments that are distracting or that create problem-solving scenarios. They should include decision making and be encouraged to take personal responsibility for their part in the development process. Coaches should adopt an autonomous yet supportive approach in working with their goalkeepers to create an environment conducive to problem solving and guided discovery. This less directed approach will often result in slower rates of learning but facilitate greater retention, autonomy and resilience in the long run, creating a mentally stronger goalkeeper.

Be open, be honest but also be compassionate. Overly critical analysis doesn't help anyone! The responsibility of the coach, initially, is to make the goalkeeper comfortable by getting him to see each obstacle and difficult situations as an opportunity and not a threat. This is done through feedback and constant support and communication as well as focusing more on the positive aspects of his game while simultaneously trying to improve the weaknesses. This approach helps to build rapport and trust. Providing feedback and reinforcing the goalkeeper's performances are just two ways the coach can help to build rapport and trust with his goalkeeper. Here are a few other suggestions on how to influence and contribute to developing the right environment for optimal learning and growth: define what success looks like, focus on the things you can control and reinforce the performance and not the outcomes.

Warrick Wood, sports psychologist at Massey University in New Zealand says it is best to "work with the athlete to define what success looks like." One suggestion in defining success is to reinforce the performance, not the outcome. This helps highlight the process as an important element, independent from winning and losing. Another step the coach can take to make the goalkeeper feel more comfortable is help him to focus on the variables he controls. This should include highlighting the importance of the goalkeeper becoming fully engaged in the performance and developing the ability to put aside

elements of competing that are outside their immediate control. Maintaining attention on the controllable elements helps the athlete focus on the present and shifts attention away from focusing on uncontrollable things like the result.

A practical way of reinforcing the performance and focusing on the controllable elements is to hold a brief review after each training session. This review should follow immediately after the training session so that the situations being discussed are still fresh in the goalkeeper's mind. In these brief reviews the coach should focus on how the goalkeeper performed the skills and decisions that were being focused on and trained regardless of the outcome that resulted from those actions or decisions. Did the goalkeeper make the correct decisions? Did they execute the skill correctly? Oftentimes a goalkeeper can make the correct decision and put himself in a great situation to make the save, execute the skill correctly and still not make the save based on the high-quality shot or an unintentional action of a teammate such as a deflection off a defender. These reviews will help to influence the mindset of the athlete to see the big picture of player development and help him focus on what he can control (i.e., his decisions and actions) and recognize the things that he cannot.

When the player feels like he has personal control over success they are more likely to exhibit greater focus and motivation to reach benchmarks and goals as well as exhibiting lower levels of anxiety. Thus, a more relaxed and ready state of mind exists and performance will likely be enhanced. Our perception of risk and failure often has a profound effect on how we respond. These perceptions may influence our decision to take on a challenge or to hide from it. How many times would you fail at something before you gave up? How would this change if you didn't view failure in a negative way?

To summarize the comfort component, psychological safety is vital to improving the goalkeeper's mental strength. Criticism and feedback are a necessity for growth but how it's delivered is the key! The coach is responsible for creating a challenging and supportive environment for the goalkeeper's growth. This includes defining success so that the player feels a greater sense of focus, motivation and control, and minimal amounts of anxiety. Secondly they must teach the goalkeeper to focus on the controllable elements, especially the process of training, playing and improving, and not focusing on the result.

This is made easier when the coach reviews and reinforces performances and not the outcomes. Mentally tough goalkeepers say that lessons learned following setbacks play a crucial role in their psychological development, although positive experiences are also important (Thelwell et al., 2010).

This highlights the importance of reflection, which can be initiated by the coach in 1-on-1 and small group meetings with the goalkeeper. It's important that the coach finds time to initiate these reflective conversations. With youth players, they could be instituted at halftime so that the goalkeeper enters the second half of the game with the correct mindset. With college or professional players, it could be done the following day in a post-match video session. This reflective process can help to build communication and understanding between the player and coach, thereby strengthening the coach–player relationship as well aiding in the technical and tactical development of the goalkeeper.

COMPETENCE LEADS TO CONFIDENCE

In addition to developing a trusting and stable relationship with the goalkeeper to provide emotional support, a coach's job is to help the goalkeeper reach a higher level. This comes from feedback on technical skills and tactical decisions, especially in the early stages of learning a new skill or technique. Accurate initial evaluations of the goalkeeper's strengths and weaknesses as well as insight into what is required at his current developmental stage and competition level are important for the coach to be able to provide the proper instruction and training activities during practice sessions.

Regardless of where the goalkeeper is on the continuum of development, repetition of the relevant skills, techniques and feedback on the decisions made by the goalkeeper in training and in games is the only way to consistently improve his play.

Through this repetition of the physical and technical skills he will imprint the movement patterns to the point of being able to perform them without thought, freeing up the goalkeeper's mind for the important decisions he needs to make while playing.

While focusing on teaching the goalkeeper his technical skills the coach is also responsible for putting him in small-sided games and training activities that will improve his recognition of common situations and scenarios that come up in competitive games. With repetition and recognition of some common patterns, these typical game scenarios slow down. This familiarity and comfort with the situations only comes about through seeing them repeatedly in training where they can be analyzed, repeated and discussed in depth. This repetition of situations helps limit confusion and panicked thinking when under pressure in games and helps increase concentration and focus because he's seen it all before.

To summarize, with consistent feedback and communication from the coach comes an understanding of the goalkeeper's roles and responsibilities. With increased skill and understanding of game situations comes a level of calm. These are two very big contributing factors to a goalkeeper's belief and confidence in his ability to get the job done. The communication and support lead to a good rapport and strong bond between the coach and his goalkeeper which adds comfort and trust to their relationship. When a goalkeeper is comfortable and competent in his skill level and understanding of the game thereby increasing his level of confidence, he exudes the most important quality that he can possibly have: presence!

DEFINING PRESENCE AND MENTAL TOUGHNESS

Countless lists exist labeling and ordering the importance of certain qualities in winning athletes. Attributes associated with mentally tough athletes include self-belief, desire, internal motivation and the ability to push the boundaries of physical and emotional pain. Remaining fully focused in the face of distractions, bouncing back from setbacks, quickly regaining emotional control after unexpected events and reframing and dealing with competition-related stress and pressure are also considered qualities of mentally tough athletes. Pressure is self-inflicted, created in our own minds and is simply a reflection of our thinking in the moment. If we are thinking about the future outcomes in the moment—if our focus is on what might happen because of our actions—we forget about the current process we must be engaged in to create success. Therefore, the ability to refrain from getting caught up in the future (i.e., the outcome) and keeping our mind focused on the present is another sign of the mentally tough athlete.

In his paper "Mental Toughness Training for Sports" written in 1982, J.E. Loehr stated that "mentally tough athletes respond in ways which enable them to remain feeling relaxed, calm and energized because they have learned to develop two skills: First, the ability to increase their flow of positive energy in crisis and adversity and second, to think in specific ways so that they have the right attitudes regarding problems, pressure, mistakes and competition." For example, Jimmy Nielsen, former professional goalkeeper with Sporting Kansas City, had an interesting way of engaging in the process of keeping himself motivated and focused throughout the long season by viewing it as a hunt or chase. He was always looking to overtake the team directly in front of us, never looking too far ahead at who was sitting in first place. Slowly but surely the team would overtake them and he would refocus his sights on the next one. By season's end the team was often on top of the table in the division. Knowing that he was this way, in the cases where the team was already on top of the table, coaches would rephrase the chase as one in which the team was in search of a certain number of points or wins. This kept him focused on what was directly in front of the team and not looking too far ahead.

Confident and mentally tough goalkeepers will exude a distinctive aura or presence which is difficult to describe as it comes through in different ways in different people, but it is very easy to see in those that have it. This definition and the descriptive adjectives describing mental toughness dovetails perfectly into the idea of presence being built on the solid foundations of comfort and competence described above. A major part of a goalkeeper's ability to remain calm and energized under pressure depends on how they view crisis and adversity. Is their attitude one of "been there done that," or one of "uh-oh...I haven't seen this before"?

Attitude has a direct link to our physiology. Why? Because performance follows attitude. Our attitude affects emotions and emotions contribute to our energy levels. One's talent determines what one can do. One's motivation determines how much one is willing to do and one's attitude determines how well one does it. Therefore, a positive, resilient mentally tough state of mind will help one thrive in the challenging world of sports. A goalkeeper will feel more capable of overcoming this adversity when he has seen it repeatedly and become comfortable with it in the training environment first. Therefore, comfort through competence—working through the process of overcoming obstacles in a repetitive and increasing nature—is one of the most important factors in creating presence and mental toughness.

In an era where the profession of soccer is advocating the decision-making skills of all players we must allow them to live with some disappointment and resolve their own problems as much as possible, while assuring them that you are available for moral support and learning opportunities. This better equips them to be mentally strong enough to deal with the situations that arise on the field when a coach has very limited ability to step in and help. Confidence is based on how you perceive a situation, what you tell yourself about how you can deal with it and, if something new is required, believing you can learn it. Finally, it requires knowing that one has prepared, in the right way, through the process of repetition and feedback. Preparation and hard work are two of the most important influences on your level of confidence. It is the knowing that one focused on the process that creates the positive results.

GOALKEEPER, COACH AND PARENT: COMMON SCENARIOS

Because the goalkeeping position is very demanding from a psychological perspective, coaches and parents are often confronted by a myriad of challenges with regard to the goalkeeper's performance and enjoyment of their role. This is especially true in the case of young goalkeepers, who are struggling with a range of social maturation issues as they try to learn the position and meet the mental demands of the position in particular. Here are a list of common concerns and cues for addressing the issues as coaches and parents.

* *Second-choice goalkeeper.* In some club situations and certainly at the high school and higher levels, teams often select a second goalkeeper. If the coach opts to play one goalkeeper either predominantly or exclusively, the second-choice goalkeeper often requires special attention. As with field players who do not get to play as much as their teammates, the second-choice goalkeeper can suffer in the areas of self-esteem and confidence, resulting in a related decrease in performance. This can lead to a range of other issues, from feeling isolated within the team to wanting to quit the team. How should coaches and parents address this issue?

1. If possible, the coach should meet with the player and parents before the season starts to explain the situation. Clarifying the second-choice status, highlighting areas to focus on to perhaps become the starter and getting early feedback as to how the player and parent will react to the situation can be very enlightening for the coach.

2. What is the role of the second-choice goalkeeper within the team? If the player has no or a poorly defined role, that player is more likely to struggle to contribute to or enjoy the experience. The coach should work hard to engender a strong bond between the goalkeepers, hoping that they will invest in one another's training, performance and enjoyment of the experience. The second-choice goalkeeper can run the warm-up (if no goalkeeper coach is available, for instance), act as a captain in training or in second-team games where appropriate, support the coaching staff on match day (gathering statistics, for instance) or perform many other roles in support of the team that all lend a sense of contribution and importance for that player.

3. Communication is critical. The coach should spend extra time with the second-choice goalkeeper every day, just checking in and giving feedback, reminding the player that they are an important part of the team. Often a bit of casual conversation about school or similar topics helps connect the player to the team and the coach and gives the coach an indicator if there is a role problem developing.

4. Help that player along and improve the team. Countless teams suffer injuries to their primary-choice goalkeepers, and the second-choice goalkeeper is rushed into service. Understanding this from a coaching perspective offers further incentive to prepare the entire goalkeeper corps for this eventuality. If the second-choice goalkeeper needs to handle crosses better to get on the field, offer to provide the extra training or work it into the team's training. The extra attention both highlights the need for improvement and also demonstrates the desire of the coach to help prepare the second-choice goalkeeper to challenge or replace the starter.

5. Get that player on the field as often as possible. Whether it's a game with a safe lead, an insurmountable deficit or just a rotation, it's important to get the second-choice goalkeeper on the field as often as possible.

- *Confidence issues.* Perhaps the most difficult issue for coaches and parents of goalkeepers is low confidence. Whether a product of inexperience, a rough match, return from injury or lay-off or some other issue, confidence is a fragile, if absolutely critical, component of effective goalkeeping. It's almost always apparent when a goalkeeper is not confident, as their performance will suffer, and they usually become detached and self-critical. Their demeanor is also visibly less assertive. Most people recognize these signs for what they are. The question is: How can coaches and parents help goalkeepers with confidence issues?

  1. First and foremost, communicate with the player. Letting a confidence issue go unaddressed is very likely to worsen the issue. If the player is exhibiting the symptoms outlined above, they're looking for help. It is important to approach the issue in a thoughtful manner. Asking the goalkeeper why they are playing poorly will not encourage them to trust the coach or parent and may further the isolation of the goalkeeper. Rather, a good approach is to ask the player

how they're doing in general and how they feel about the team's performance. Often this will lead to the goalkeeper opening up about their own concerns about their individual performance level. Sometimes just talking about the confidence issue—identifying it—will help. Other times, a deeper discussion is necessary. Regardless, developing a base of resilient confidence is part of the process of increasing mental toughness outlined earlier in the chapter.

2. As a rule, try to get the goalkeeper to focus on what they control. If a goalkeeper is lacking confidence because the team has been steam-rolled in successive matches, there may not be a great deal the goalkeeper could have done to prevent the routs. However, building the discussion around the goalkeeper's training, mental preparation, relationship with the defense and so on helps the player focus on variables that can be controlled.

3. For coaches, put the goalkeeper in training environments designed to increase the goalkeeper's confidence, whether through a focus on an area of concern (e.g., high balls) or where they get a lot of time on the ball and have significant help (e.g., a playing environment with restarts chipped in to the goalkeeper and the starting back line playing together in front of the goalkeeper).

4. Always simplify. Goalkeepers with confidence issues often have multiple concerns: their preparation, the defense, the standings, their scholarship, off-field issues. Help the player get back to why they play goalkeeper: The chance to make saves, play an important role, enjoy their time with their teammates, compete for a championship and so on. Focus on making the first save, making the right calls for the defense, making better distribution, helping the team get a win and so on. It's easier to isolate a couple of these, get them right and then build from there. Confidence increases with each goal achieved.

-   *Failure.* When the goalkeeper does fail, it is often in a very glaring way. The goalkeeper plays a very visible, specialized position and one that can very decisively influence the success or failure of the entire team. If the failure was something the goalkeeper could control (e.g., goals resulting from poor handling, getting chipped because one is out of position), the pain can be very real for the goalkeeper. As a parent or coach, what do we say to goalkeepers after they fail?

1. Particularly with children, it is very important that adults do not criticize or excoriate a player who fails on a given day. Life is full of failure, and one of the lessons of goalkeeping is that sometimes one's shortcomings are there for the world to see.

2. That said, every goalkeeper and person deals with failure in their own way. Some players, particularly senior youth and professional players, can be told in fairly blunt terms that they need to improve their performance. However, for younger players in particular, the emphasis has to be on learning from their mistakes and on understanding that their response to failure is more of a measure than the failure itself. Working through failure is part of focusing on process rather than outcome.

3. Help them talk through their performance when they are ready. Try to be fair, pointing out their positive contributions to the team, and also helping them understand their shortcomings, and that if they gave their best effort, they did not fail.

4. Did they control the variables they could control? Did they train hard to prepare? Did they give full effort?

5. Think in terms of helping them be proactive. If they were beaten on a cross, encourage them to set a goal to improve on dealing with crosses the next season.

- *Body language.* Closely related to the confidence issue is the idea of body language. More than any player on the field, the body language shared by the goalkeeper affects the team. A confident, assertive goalkeeper stiffens a defense and helps a team achieve its goals. Conversely, a goalkeeper with a sullen presence can undermine the confidence of the entire back line or team. A combative goalkeeper who gesticulates wildly to officials and opponents and lacks focus can become a distraction and also undermine confidence. How, then, to strike the right tone?

  1. Most goalkeepers do not have any idea what sort of image they portray.

  2. Coaches are often aware if their goalkeeper is not leading through their body language, but very few address the issue. Parents may be concerned about their child's demeanor, but often find children do not want to talk about this issue with their parents.

3.   The best teaching tool in this case is video. Film the goalkeeper throughout a training session or match, not focusing on the other players or the action per se, just the goalkeeper. Many players are shocked at what they see when they watch themselves. In fact, it's best not to accuse the goalkeeper of unproductive body language, but to just ask them what they see. Do they seem positive? Are they actively involved? Are they leading? In this way, there is guided discovery of the image the goalkeeper is building within the team, and the chance to discuss ways to create a more positive, confident leader at the back.

4.   Another means of getting at the body language issue is to have the goalkeeper watch professional goalkeepers on television. Ask them questions about the goalkeeper's demeanor. Are they confident? Assertive? Again, this type of exploration allows the goalkeeper to observe the right body language without having to be defensive about their own demeanor. In fact, it is clear in our culture that imitation is a prevalent form of expression, and imitating the desired successful behaviors and demeanor is part of maturation.

•   *Blame and responsibility.* Another stage of learning and maturing for young goalkeepers is the issue of deciding blame when failure happens. Many goalkeepers—rightly or wrongly—blame their back line or a specific player for the break down, or blame the team for not scoring, or the coach for playing the wrong players and so on. In this way, they deflect or deny their own responsibility. This can be a very difficult situation to cope with—particularly for parents, who tend to get more direct and forceful feedback—as the effort must be directed at trying to get away from the blame or responsibility issue and onto how to prevent the situation from happening again.

1.   The best point of intervention in this case is often to assure that the conversation does not happen in front of the team, which can lead to accusations that erode chemistry.

2.   Begin by encouraging the player to air it out, sharing their viewpoint on what happened. Often, it's some variation on, "She didn't mark her player and I told her and she refused and blamed me when the girl was left open and scored

and now we lost and everyone thinks it's my fault." This is a lot to process, and whatever is said, it's typically very defensive and designed to create a victim portrayal to shift blame. Occasionally more mature players will start down this road and realize what they're doing in mid-stream and shut it down, beginning the road to learning. Younger players, particularly teenagers, tend to be more intractable.

3. Regardless of the merits of the story, the goal here is to get to the real issue. Why did we give up a goal or lose? How do we learn from this? Anson Dorrance, the World Cup and 21-time NCAA National Championship coach at the University of North Carolina, frequently reminds his players that while victory has readily identifiable mothers and fathers, failure is an orphan. No one wants the blame. Yet Dorrance continuously reminds his players that every goal conceded has numerous antecedents and mothers. Was there pressure on the ball that was served over the back line? Were duels lost? Did everyone complete their marking assignment? Did the goalkeeper perform adequately? A constructive discussion with the goalkeeper often reveals that blame, if it need be allotted, can be spread out all over the field.

4. Part of the hoped-for outcome of these discussions is learning life lessons, particularly to look to oneself in assessing blame and responsibility rather than lashing out at or in any way blaming others. Most players know when they have failed. Goalkeepers, because their failures are very visible, tend to react defensively to failure and often do not want to shoulder blame by themselves. If the goalkeeper can take a moment and assess their own actions and then work with coaches and teammates to learn from their collective mistakes in a given situation, blame can be dispatched in favor of collective responsibility and the opportunity to learn and improve.

•   *Off-field issues.* One of the more difficult concerns to diagnose for a coach occurs when goalkeepers have off-field issues. Whether it's academic difficulty, substance abuse, a family concern or a psychological condition (e.g., depression), these concerns can be masked to varying degrees by players, and in some cases they may be fiercely determined not to let the issue affect their play or share their pain with their coach or parent. Indeed, many young people find sports to be their escape from their stressors, and do not want to admit there is an issue affecting their performance. Yet these concerns can have serious consequences for both the individual and the team, on the field and off. Sometimes coaches and parents will be completely unaware there is an issue. How do coaches detect and deal with off-field issues affecting their players?

1. As with all of these scenarios, communication is vital to recognizing and assisting players with off-field issues. Developing healthy, daily interaction with players builds trust and it may be that the child will open up to the coach because of that trust and allow the process of helping and healing to commence.

2. Thorough communication means staying in touch with parents and teachers as well as paying attention to team dynamics throughout the season. Often, the warning signs of academic difficulty will be noticed and shared by teachers before a progress report is forwarded to the coach. If the coach and teacher can work together to enhance the performance of the child in the classroom, the player will likely enjoy their soccer experience more as well. Within the team, it sometimes becomes apparent that a player is becoming isolated or is being bullied (for instance), and the coach can be proactive in assuring a safe, positive environment for all team members by monitoring team dynamics.

3. Make use of all available support. Often coaches are unsure of what to do if they suspect a player has an off-field issue. Ignoring any issue is a disservice to the person, and coaches have a duty to try to make use of any resources that can help improve the life and experience of the player in question. It is important to stress that the coach should not be an independent actor in aiding players with off-field issues. Parents and school officials should be made aware of any suspicion that a player is struggling with an off-field issue and all should be part of the planning (along with the player where appropriate) to help the player overcome the issue.

In conclusion, goalkeepers are by definition under considerable pressure. Coaches and parents can work together with the player to help recognize and overcome a wide range of issues to improve the experience and performance of the player. Communication, recognition and a patient, thoughtful approach that emphasizes learning and trust will most help the player enjoy their soccer, and also reach their potential.

05

CHAPTER 5

THE TRAINING GUIDE: EXERCISES BY THEME

GROUP WARM-UP

Group warm-up.

Place goalkeepers in a grid with a goalkeeper-to-ball ratio of 2:1. Goalkeepers move around the area (no standing) and randomly exchange the balls. Emphasize that all movement, distribution and receiving must be done using goalkeeper techniques.

Progression

1. Balls are rolled underhand and picked up by the receiving goalkeeper.
2. Balls are bounced and caught by the receiving goalkeeper.
3. Balls are chest-passed from goalkeeper to goalkeeper.
4. Balls are tossed underhand in an arc for the receiving goalkeeper to go up and catch (high balls).
5. Balls are set down for another goalkeeper to collapse dive and cover.

SHADOW GOALKEEPING

sports-graphics.com

Shadow goalkeeping.

A coach or goalkeeper leads the group through footwork and diving. The leader stands out in front and the remainder of the group mimic his goalkeeper movements. This is a fun way for larger groups of young players to learn about basic movements and diving.

Included elements
1. Basic stance
2. Shuffling left and right
3. Backpedaling
4. Creeping forward (closing down)
5. Diving left and right
6. Falling down onto one's back and recovering
7. Falling down onto one's front side and recovering
8. Jumping up to catch a phantom high ball

PAIRS' FOOTWORK AND HANDLING WARM-UP

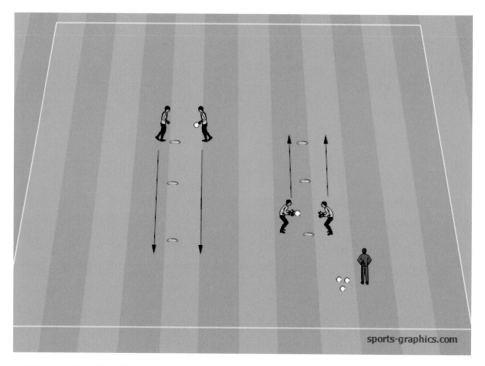

Pairs' footwork and handling warm-up.

Goalkeepers work in pairs along two parallel lines of cones, each 12 yards in length. In the first phase, goalkeepers chest-pass a ball as they shuffle down the length of one cone line. As shown above, they then prepare to shuffle back down the adjacent line. Emphasize working at a smooth, reasonable pace—it's not a race, and the footwork should be clean throughout.

Progression

Pairs' footwork and handling warm-up: One ball.

1. The goalkeepers bounce-pass the ball to one another.

Pairs' footwork and handling warm-up: Two balls, one goalkeeper chest-passing and one bounce-passing.

2. Add a second ball. One goalkeeper chest-passes and the other bounce-passes. Goalkeepers need to pass simultaneously and work together to build rhythm in their footwork, service and handling.

3. With two balls, one goalkeeper chest-passes and the other passes below waist height. The balls should not touch the ground.

STICKS FOOTWORK AND HANDLING WARM-UP

Sticks footwork and handling warm-up (1).

The working goalkeeper starts in the ready position between the sticks. He performs footwork around one of the sticks and returns to the center of the goal, where he saves a serve from the other goalkeeper. This is a flexible, efficient warm-up combining goalkeeper movements with various handling elements.

Variations
1. Figure 8 footwork and save.
2. Add a cross-over step to the start of the footwork.
3. Shots on the ground.
4. Volleyed shots or half-volleyed shots.
5. Goalkeeper does a push-up to start each sequence.

Sticks footwork and handling warm-up (2).

Sticks footwork and handling warm-up (3).

GAME DAY WARM-UP

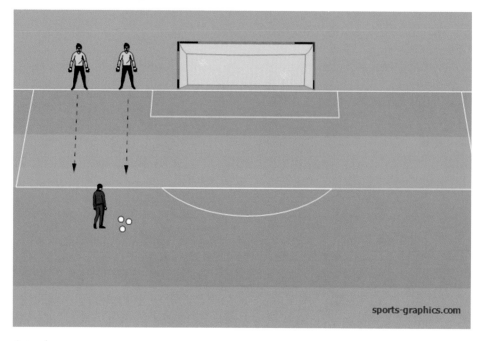

Game day warm-up.

An example of a goalkeeper movement warm-up routine. This progression can be combined with handling and shot-stopping to ready the goalkeepers for match play.

Progression

1. Jog to the top of the 18-yard box and back to the end line twice.
2. High knees to the top of the 18-yard box and back to the end line twice.
3. High heels to the top of the 18-yard box and back to the end line twice.
4. Shuffle to the top of the 18-yard box and back to the end line twice.
5. Run at three-quarters speed to the top of the 18-yard box and backpedal to the end line twice.
6. Bounce a ball and skip to the top of the 18-yard box and back to the end line twice.
7. Bounce a ball, toss and catch a high ball to the top of the 18-yard box and back to the end line twice.

MOVEMENT

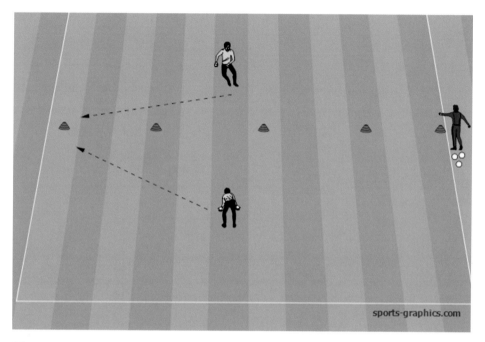

Mirrors.

This is a simple environment wherein young goalkeepers can focus on their footwork and senior goalkeepers can be drilled at pace to move throughout their area. As the exercise name implies, one player leads and the other goalkeeper mirrors their partner's movement. All movement must be from the goalkeeper's stance position and be goalkeeper footwork (e.g., shuffling to the sides, backpedaling, crouching and moving forward). At this level, each player should lead for thirty seconds. The coach should monitor the players' movement, controlling speed and looking for clean footwork, particularly as they tire.

ZIG-ZAG SHUFFLE

Zig-zag shuffle.

This is a great way to train goalkeepers to move laterally back and forth across the goal. Goalkeepers shuffle through a zig-zag of towels or cones. Focus on short chop steps, never allowing the feet to click together (i.e., balance and change of direction are impaired).

Progression
1. Work backward through the towels.
2. Toss a ball for the goalkeeper to catch. They must set their feet before making the save.

CANS FOOTWORK AND SAVE

Cans footwork and save (1).

The goalkeeper does footwork through various set-ups of cones or other obstacles (e.g., inverted cans) and proceeds to a stick goal to save a shot. It is important to be creative with training to provide some variety as goalkeepers work to master and sustain skills.

Variations

1. Goalkeeper shuffles through the cans, gets through the gates, sets and saves.
2. Goalkeeper faces away from the sticks and shuffles backward through the cans, goes to goal and saves.
3. Goalkeeper shuffles completely around each of the cans, then goes to the goal and saves.
4. Goalkeeper shuffles and then dives between each of the cans, then gets to goal and saves.

Cans footwork and save (2).

HANDLING

Individual handling progression.

Goalkeepers' hands are similar in importance to their performance as field players' feet (W catching position shown above). Consequently, the keepers need hundreds of touches at every session to remain sharp. The following progression allows individual goalkeepers to get quick, intensive touch training. This progression should be performed frequently, particularly for young goalkeepers as they develop touch and confidence on the ball. Each of the movements in the progression should be performed for twenty seconds at intensive pace.

Progression
1. Push the ball back and forth between the hands at eye height. The contact points should be the fingers, not the palms.

2. Widen the hands to beyond shoulder width and continue to toss and catch from one hand to the other.

3. Raise the hands above the head and continue to toss and catch from one hand to the other.

4. Cup the ball and straighten the arm. Rotate the extended arm around behind the back, stretching while controlling the ball. Move from side to side, reaching to raise the height of the ball at the peak of the rotation (stretch).

5. Spread the legs beyond shoulder width and rotate the ball around one leg, starting at the knee and working down to the ankle and back up (stretch). Work both legs.

6. Put the ball on the ground and use the finger tips to rotate the ball around both feet in a figure-8 pattern. Reverse direction after ten seconds.

7. Complete a figure-8 pattern at knee height (around the knees), working the ball with the hands as fast and clean as possible.

8. Handling challenge #1. Put both hands together cradling the ball behind the knees (reach around the outside of the legs). Toss the ball up, moving the hands around the legs and catch the ball with the hands in front of the legs. Emphasize soft, cradling catches without any noise or juggle. Repeat as quickly as possible.

9. Handling challenge #2. Put both hands together cradling the ball with one hand in front of the legs and one behind. Toss the ball upward and reverse the position of the hands, catching the ball on its way down. Again, emphasize quiet, soft catches. Repeat as quickly as possible.

10. Sit down and work the ball back and forth through the legs while making a pedaling motion with the legs. The feet should not touch the ground and the goalkeeper should lean back slightly as he works.

11. Lying on his back, the goalkeeper throws the ball in the air with two hands and tries to get to his feet and catch the ball before it hits the ground. Repeat as often as possible in thirty seconds.

12. Lying on his front side, the goalkeeper throws the ball in the air with two hands and tries to get to his feet and catch the ball before it hits the ground. Repeat as often as possible in thirty seconds.

13. Bounce the ball and catch. Bounce the ball at pace and catch the ball with proper (i.e., W) hand position.

14. Bounce the ball and catch while moving it around (e.g., behind a heel, at one's side).

15. Walk and bounce the ball and catch.

16. Skip and bounce the ball and catch.

17. Skip and bounce the ball. Stop and toss the ball in the air and go up and catch the ball at its highest point.

18. Hammer fist. Walk and bounce and catch the ball. Every third repetition, use the fist to punch the ball to the ground and recover the ball.

PAIRS' HANDLING

The following are options for efficient, challenging pairs handling for goalkeepers. Pairs stand two yards apart. In each case, emphasize quality over quantity (do not hurry). Train each variation for thirty seconds.

1. Chest-toss and catch. Throw the ball back and forth, working on extending the hands to catch and looking at the ball after the catch is made.

2. Short-hop receiving. The ball is thrown overhand and to bounce just in front of the target's feet. Work on catching the short hop cleanly without backing up.

3. Ground pick-up. Roll the ball back and forth and pick it up by staggering the feet, dipping the trailing knee to close up the space so the ball cannot get through and tucking the elbows behind the ball as one makes the save (stand 7 yards apart for this variation). Step forward after the catch.

4. High-ball catch. One goalkeeper tosses underhand, providing a lofted ball for the other goalkeeper to catch. Jump from one foot, driving the other knee high to increase the height of the jump. The hands are extended to catch the ball at the highest possible point and in front of the head. When the ball is secured, it is held high above the head while the feet are reestablished on the ground. The serving goalkeeper runs forward to challenge the receiving goalkeeper at the point of the catch.

5.   Punt and catch. From a distance of four yards, punt the ball for the partner to catch.

6.   Two-ball catch #1. One goalkeeper bounce-passes the ball while the other chest-passes the ball as the two interchange balls at the same time. Focus on clean handling.

7. Two-ball catch #2. One goalkeeper chest-passes the ball and the other throws the ball underhand at knee-height to the other goalkeeper. Passes are simultaneous and can be played with more pace for advanced goalkeepers. Focus on clean handling throughout.

8. Two-ball catch #3. Goalkeepers stand three yards apart and staggered in alignment. Both players toss the ball underhand and straight, and then shuffle sideways to receive their partner's serve.

BALLS AND STRIKES

Balls and strikes.

Two goalkeepers stand ten yards apart. Players alternate throwing the ball at one another as hard as they can. Any ball that is delivered between the knees and head, and between the shoulders of the receiving goalkeeper that is not handled cleanly (i.e., dropped or bobbled) results in a strike. All throws outside of that zone are balls. Balls do not accumulate. The first player to three strikes loses. Adjust the distance between players to suit the ability of the players.

PAIRS' ONE-HAND THROW AND CATCH

Pairs' one-hand throw and catch.

Two goalkeepers stand four yards apart and throw the ball to one another. Goalkeepers toss underhand and the ball needs to be served at chest-height or higher so the goalkeeper can catch with one hand and the wrist facing downward. Alternate the catching hand. This exercise forces a young goalkeeper to concentrate on the act of catching and creates soft hands.

Progression
1. Overhand tosses.
2. More distance between goalkeepers.

PAIRS' PUNCHING AND BOXING

At the beginning level, teach punching and boxing to introduce proper technique, emphasizing that these saves are to be used in emergency situations. Start with one player serving underhand to the other goalkeeper, who starts in a seated position. Punching involves using clenched fists to push a ball away.

Progression

1. Sitting. The server tosses balls underhand for the goalkeeper to punch. The goalkeeper initiates each sequence by leaning slightly back (to emphasize using all of the muscles from the lower back on up to gain power in the punch) and then punching through the back lower half of the ball to push it back up to the server.

2. Kneeling. This progression helps young goalkeepers learn to push through the punch save. The server stands four yards away and serves underhand to the active goalkeeper. Once again, the goalkeeper initiates each sequence by leaning back and then pushing forward through the serve. The goalkeeper should follow through by pushing forward down onto their front side.

3. Standing. The goalkeeper works from a standing position. Serves are underhand and above shoulder height.

4. Add a standing player for the goalkeeper to punch over. The server tosses balls just above the standing player's head for the goalkeeper to jump and punch.

BOXING

Use the same progression (sitting, kneeling, standing, jumping with a player to box over) to teach boxing. Boxing is similar to punching but using a single fist. Once again, this save is taught as an emergency measure.

SHARP MOVEMENT AND HANDLING

Sharp movement and handling.

This exercise adds movement to handling. The goalkeeper starts in his ready position in the center area of the goal. He moves quickly behind the dummy and clears to deal with a serve at pace from the first server. Then he quickly recovers behind the dummy to make a save on the second shot from the other server. The two servers can focus on different and rotating shot types (e.g., high, low, at pace, shots to tip) and the goalkeeper can be put through forward rolls or footwork before each sequence if a more challenging environment is desired.

DISTRIBUTION

Four's distribution.

This activity uses a club warm-up environment where groups of goalkeepers can train efficiently in the areas of distribution and receiving. Players roll the ball to the opposite line and then go to the back of their own line. Focus on reaching down to the ground to release the ball with no bounce and on proper receiving technique.

Progression

1. Players throw the ball to the opposite line. Tosses should be at chest-height, focusing on proper throwing technique.
2. Players skip-pass the ball to the opposite line for the first goalkeeper to receive. The technique here is to get the ball there faster than a rolled throw but also deliver the ball to the feet of the target (unlike a thrown ball). Bring the ball by the shoulder with the elbow bent. Drop the shoulder on the throwing side and release the ball at a low point while pushing the fingers underneath the ball at the moment of release to create backspin and keep the ball low to the ground for the receiving player.
3. Players punt the ball to the first player in the other line.
4. Players drop-kick the ball to the first player in the other line.

SOCCER
GOALKEEPER
TRAINING

FOUR CORNERS DISTRIBUTION

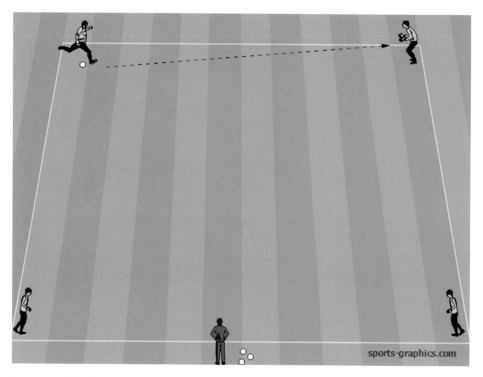

Four corners distribution.

In this club distribution and pick-up exercise, goalkeepers receive from set position and distribute in a clockwise, counter-clockwise or random fashion. Emphasize proper technique on both the distributing and receiving ends. Adjust the size of the grid to fit the age and ability of the goalkeepers. Add a second ball for skilled groups.

Progression

1. Players roll the ball to the target and pick up.
2. Players skip-pass the ball to the target. Emphasize a low release point, throwing the ball about 2/3 of the distance to the target.
3. Players throw the ball, baseball-style, to the next target.
4. Players pass the ball (with their feet) to the next target. Goalkeepers also use their feet to receive in this stage of the exercise.

5.   Players punt the ball to the next target.

6.   Players drop-kick the ball to the next target.

PUNTING INTO THE GOAL

Punting into the goal.

This simple exercise should be repeated at training on a weekly basis so that goalkeepers become comfortable with punting and drop-kicking the ball at a young age. Key technical points include consistent footwork, hand release and striking, good balance, a strong back-swing and follow-through and learning to land on the kicking foot on the follow-through.

GOAL KICKS

Goal kicks.

The goalkeeper practices hitting goal kicks over the top of the goal from the penalty kick spot. Use a large ball supply. The idea here is that balls lofted or chipped over the goal on a consistent basis will simulate successful goal kicks. Often, using the goal provides a visual for the goalkeeper to help him push the ball over the top. Indeed, it is useful to think of the exercise as a bad shooting exercise. Practice hitting balls with both feet. As the goalkeeper improves his service, move the start point to the "D" and beyond.

PAIRS' BACK-PASSES IN A GRID

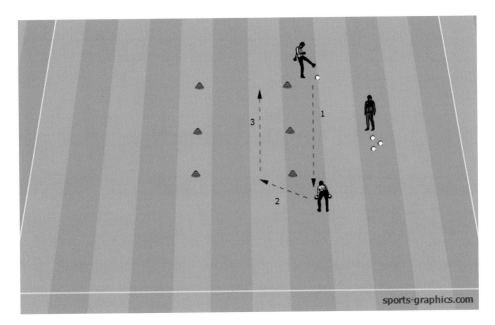

sports-graphics.com

Pairs' back-passes in a grid.

This is a very efficient environment for teaching young goalkeepers the need to sharply change the angle of play when they receive a ball on the ground. The ball is passed between goalkeepers. The ball must be played back in two touches and in a lane other than the one in which it is received.

Cues
1. The first touch is positive (played forward).
2. The first touch is played outside the hips (change the angle).
3. Receive with the inside of one foot and play with the inside of either foot.
4. Learn to become proficient with both feet.
5. It is critical to reset to a deep starting position after passing so that good angles forward can be set for the receiving touch.
6. How accurate are the passes? The goalkeeper should be able to hold the foot at the end of the follow-through after passing to show the intended path of the ball.

Variations

1. Heavier pace on the passing.

2. Every other pass in the air (volley or settle).

3. Add an attacker who randomly follows some back-passes to pressure goalkeeper.

CLEARANCES

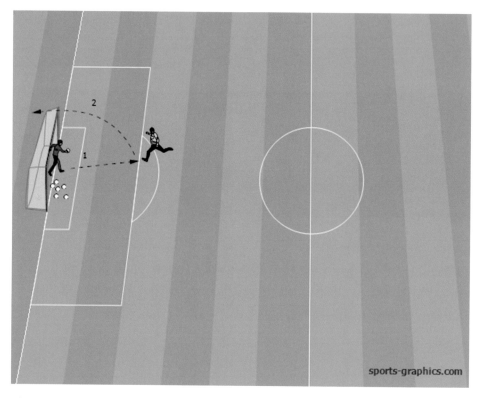

sports-graphics.com

Clearances.

This exercise helps the goalkeeper learn to deal with balls rolling or bouncing near the area that have to be cleared, both without and with pressure. Turning the exercise toward the goal helps the goalkeeper learn to play the ball high (over the top of the goal) and for distance.

Variations

1. Balls rolled at varying pace from the server. Two-touch clearances.
2. Balls rolled at varying pace from the server. One-touch clearances.
3. Balls bounced in at varying pace from the server. Two-touch clearances.
4. Balls bounced in at varying pace from the server. One-touch clearances.
5. Any of the above variations with light pressure from the server, who follows his pass.

DIVING

Pairs' diving progression.

One goalkeeper kneels and the other faces him with a ball ready to serve. The active goalkeeper dives left, then right, gobbling up and returning ground serves from his partner.

Points of emphasis

1. Contact points: Outside of knee, outside of hips, outside of shoulder.
2. Top leg bent for protection and recoil after save.
3. Bottom leg straight.
4. Ball held using both hands with the top hand on the top of the ball and the bottom hand on the back (ground is the third hand).
5. Ball held well in front of eyes, with bent arms.
6. Dive angle forward.

Progression

1. Tossed underhand serves. (Goalkeeper kneeling)
2. Bounced serves. (Goalkeeper kneeling)
3. Ground serves. (Goalkeeper standing)
4. Tossed underhand serves. (Goalkeeper standing)
5. Bounced underhand serves. (Goalkeeper standing)

Variations

1. Serve from feet.
2. Use a medicine ball (U14 and older goalkeepers).

SWITCH DIVE

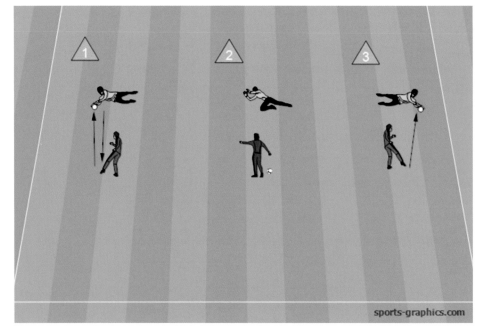

Switch dive.

The coach serves a ball for the goalkeeper to dive to his right and save (1). The goalkeeper rolls the ball back to the server but stays down on his right side (2). At a command from the coach, he quickly rotates his hips and dives to his left to save a serve to that side from the coach. The idea here is that the coach controls the sequence and can make coaching points and also compel the goalkeeper to change sides very quickly to save.

THREE'S DIVING PROGRESSION

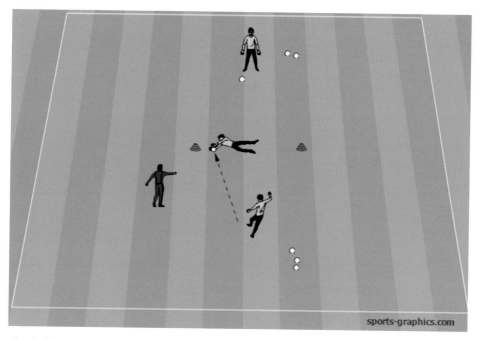

Three's diving progression.

This is a very efficient way to train diving. Using a cone goal and two servers, one on each side of the cone goal, the servers alternate passing the ball for the goalkeeper to dive and save. After each save, the goalkeeper recovers and faces the other server. Note that all serves should be toward the same cone to assure that the goalkeeper trains diving in both directions.

Progression

1. Service on the ground.
2. Service in the air.
3. Bounced serves.
4. Widen the goal. Extension diving (ground, air and bounced serves).

DIVE AND RECOVER

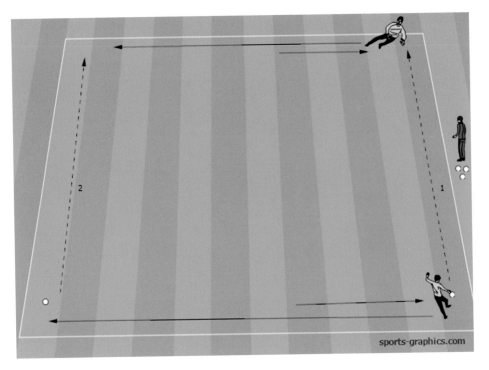

Dive and recover.

Two goalkeepers work on opposite ends of the grid, starting at the center point of their line. The near goalkeeper (shooter) moves to his right to the corner of the grid and passes the ball on the ground for his partner on the other end to dive to his left and save. After the save, the goalkeeper leaves the ball at the corner. The shooter then runs across to his left and plays the second ball straight across to the goalkeeper's right side. The goalkeeper recovers from the first save and moves across his line to dive and save on his right. Again, the goalkeeper leaves the ball at the corner after the save and both goalkeepers return to the center of their end lines. They now change roles and play the other way. Play for two minutes, focusing on proper technique with every dive and clean movement between saves.

Progression

- Serves on the ground.
- Serves in the air.
- Cones, hurdles or ladders for footwork before each save.
- Place cones four yards inside each corner. The goalkeeper preparing to dive must remain at the cone until the ball is struck by his partner (extension diving).
- Start with two balls at each of the active corners. The first shot forces a diving save from the keeper and then the second follows, forcing a recovery save.

GOALKEEPER TAKES BALL DIVING

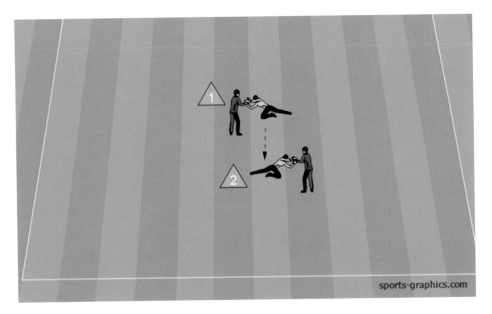

sports-graphics.com

Goalkeeper takes ball diving.

Use two servers if possible. The goalkeeper alternates diving from his feet to the left and right. In each case, the coach holds the ball for the goalkeeper to take with the dive. The coach can move the ball to work on high or low saves, and another useful tip is for the coach to back off at the last second, compelling the goalkeeper to dive forward to take the ball.

FORWARD DIVE ANGLE

Forward dive angle.

This exercise is used to compel the goalkeeper to dive at a forward angle, getting him to the ball earlier, and reaching more balls through the aggressive angle. In introducing the exercise, explain that clean footwork is used from the start point to the central cone. From there, explain that the goalkeeper steps into the goal and that the outside post has been moved forward to compel the goalkeeper to dive forward to keep the ball from entering the goal. Note that the exercise can be run in either direction (left- or right-side diving). This set-up can also be used to train low tipping.

Forward dive angle.

Progression

1. Serves on the ground.

2. Bounced serves.

3. Serves in the air (shin- to chest-height).

4. Extension diving (lengthen the goal).

TWO-BALL DIVING

Two-ball diving.

This exercise is an excellent means of warming up the goalkeeper's diving before a finishing session or as a reminder of the importance of handling in diving. The working goalkeeper lies on his side, ready to cover a ball placed at front of his shoulders at arm's-length distance. The server stands two yards away from and at eye level to the working goalkeeper. The working goalkeeper initiates the sequence by covering the near ball, which is the signal for the server to ping the ball toward the goalkeeper on the ground and at eye-height or beyond. The working goalkeeper saves (see above), returns and the sequence repeats. Work both sides, typically for 25-30 seconds each.

DIVING SQUARE

Diving square.

This exercise is a grueling workout for up to five goalkeepers, each of whom start at the midpoint of one side of an eight-yard square. Place a ball at each corner of the square near the cones and on the side where the goalkeepers will dive (see diagram). At a signal from the coach, the goalkeepers dive in the same direction and cover the ball on their line. They then rotate one position left or right (all move in the same direction). When all goalkeepers have reached their start position, the group dive and cover again and the exercise continues. Work in one direction for one minute and then reverse directions. If a fifth goalkeeper is present, he waits near the coach and then jumps in after the closest goalkeeper completes his dive (a built-in rest).

Diving square.

Variations

1. The exercise is a race. When one goalkeeper works fast enough to tag the next goalkeeper in the direction he is working, he wins.

2. Add three push-ups for each goalkeeper each time they move to the next side of the square.

3. Add two burpees for each goalkeeper each time they move to the next side of the grid.

4. Put an attacker at each ball. This player pushes on the ball with his foot as the goalkeeper covers the ball.

1-VS.-1 SITUATIONS

Closing down. The goalkeeper moves toward the attacker, focusing on longer steps while the ball is out of the feet of the player and shorter steps as the distance closes. Note the posture of the goalkeeper–'big', to cover as much goal as possible as he moves.

1-VS.-1 IN A LANE

1-vs.-1 in a lane.

Use a narrow grid (5 × 8 yards) to teach closing down. Explain that the breakaway is being inverted in the sense that this exercise looks at the final stage of closing down. An attacker begins at the far side of the grid with the ball while the goalkeeper is ready at the near end of the grid. On the first touch from the attacker, the goalkeeper begins to close down, using a longer step or two and then short steps (so as to be able to adjust). Hands are lower than the set position at the sides. In the first phase, the attacker's second touch is long and the goalkeeper covers the ball. Focus on the movement, reading the touch and quality of the covering technique.

Progression

1. The attacker can dribble, but cannot shoot, and he tries to get past the goalkeeper and over the end line. The goalkeeper searches for a touch that allows him to take away the ball. Focus on getting into the feet of the attacker.

2. The attacker takes a touch and then looks up and takes a longer touch as he brings the leg up and back (preparing to shoot). These cues compel the goalkeeper to take a set-step, setting his feet and preparing to save. The attacker continues to dribble (no shooting).

3. The attacker must play at full speed. Focus on closing space while watching for cues that the attacker will shoot. Choose to block or cover depending on the position of the ball.

BLOCKING LINE

Blocking line.

The active goalkeeper first successively covers each of the balls in the line while the attacker pushes on the ball as the keeper covers. Work in both directions. Focus on extending the hands, keeping proper hand placement (top and back), absorbing pressure from the attacker's challenge, stretching the body out behind the ball and holding the ball at eye-height. Train in both directions. Work for both speed and quality throughout.

Progression

1. Any rebounds have to be covered immediately.
2. The attacker tries to arrive at the ball at the same time as the goalkeeper, forcing a block and cover.
3. The attacker tries to arrive just before the goalkeeper, who has to get close and block.

Blocking line.

BREAKAWAYS

Breakaways.

Attackers practice breakaways, starting 25 yards from goal. The attackers must run at speed and cannot turn back. The goalkeeper focuses on closing, getting control of the situation by limiting the attacker's options and spreading to save. Periodically change the angle of the run from the attacker to allow the goalkeeper to deal with different runs.

Breakaway or through-ball?

This is similar to the breakaway exercise, except that the player in the right-hand serving line above can either pass to the attacker in the left-side line (in which a breakaway ensues) or push the ball between the attacker and the goalkeeper, resulting in a through-ball. The goalkeeper must read the pass and decide whether to go for the ball or deal with the breakaway. To further complicate the scenario, allow the server to join the play as a recovering defender. He must work with the goalkeeper to cut out the run and the ball from the attacker.

GOALKEEPER CHALLENGE

Goalkeeper challenge.

Use two goals, twenty yards apart. One goalkeeper, the attacker, starts with his hand on the ball, twelve yards from goal. The defending goalkeeper is three yards away. When the attacker takes his hand off of the ball, the duel is live. The attacker may not shoot with his first touch. The defender must decide when and whether to attack and try to win the ball.

K-STOP

K-stop: Technical.

This is a specialized save for dealing with shooters near the goal where the goalkeeper has the opportunity to get in tight to the attacker and block the shot. In the diagram above, the goalkeeper starts in a seated position (1) and works to a K position on one knee with the near-side arm and hand extended to create as big a shape as possible to block the shot from the coach, who drives a ball at the goalkeeper. Work on going to both sides.

K-stop: Near post.

This exercise puts the K-stop into a functional setting. The goalkeeper begins by covering his near-post near the server. As the ball is passed to the attacker in front of goal, the goalkeeper closes and goes to a K-stop pose. Emphasize getting close to the ball before getting down. Train both posts. To keep the goalkeeper honest, the server on the end line should periodically try to score rather than pass to the attacker.

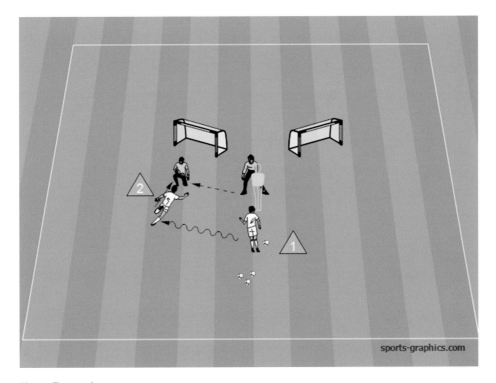

K-stop: Two goals.

The goalkeeper starts behind the dummy, opposite the attacker with the ball (1). The attacker waits and baits the goalkeeper to one side and the other before dribbling at speed across the face of either small goal. The goalkeeper must follow, close with the shooter and use a K-stop to block the shot at goal. The attacker cannot slow down or change directions once he commits to one side.

LOW TIPPING

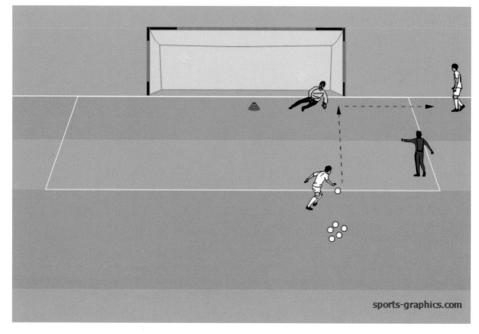

sports-graphics.com

Low tipping progression.

This is an efficient environment for training low tipping. The coach serves balls to the active goalkeeper who attempts to tip the ball to the target player. That player returns the ball to the coach and the cycle repeats. Be sure to train low tipping on both sides.

Progression

1. Ground serves. (Goalkeeper kneeling)
2. Ground serves. (Goalkeeper standing)
3. Low serves. (Goalkeeper kneeling)
4. Low serves. (Goalkeeper standing)
5. Add movement: The goalkeeper starts at the near post, shuffles to the center cone and then moves back toward the post and tips the ball wide.

Low tipping (1).

Emphasize clean technique. Note the contact points for the dive (hip and shoulder) and the importance of meeting the ball with the arm bent and the contact point (the base of the fingers or the base of the hand for power).

Low tipping (2).

The follow-through is critical for strong tipping. The eyes travel with the ball to insure accurate tipping and the arm extends fully in the direction the ball is being pushed.

SOCCER
GOALKEEPER
TRAINING

PING-PONG LOW TIPPING

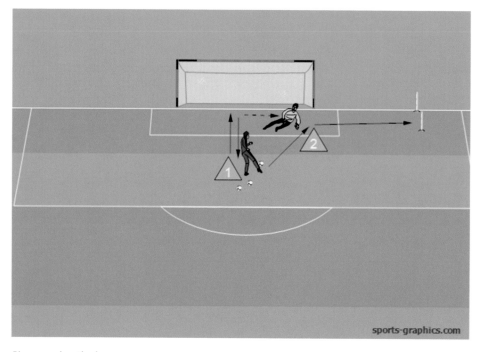

Ping-pong low tipping.

The coach and goalkeeper knock a ball back-and-forth, playing one- and two-touch. The coach decides when to shoot a ball low toward the post and the goalkeeper must dive and tip the ball wide, attempting to push the ball through the stick goal as in the diagram. This exercise compels the goalkeeper to focus on the passing until he must quickly get down and tip the ball away, creating realistic training pressure. Work one side and then the other, or, for more advanced goalkeepers, the coach can shoot to either side.

DEALING WITH HIGH BALLS

Technical high catching.

Progression

1. Bounce the ball; toss above the head and catch and hold above and in front of the head.

2. Walk and bounce the ball; toss the ball and call "Keeper!"; catch above and in front of the head. Hold the ball at the catching position while stabilizing the body at landing and demonstrate control.

3. Walk and bounce the ball; toss and call "Keeper!"; jump from one foot, propelling the other knee (bent) high to maximize the jump and also for protection; catch the ball above and in front of the head; hold the ball at the point of contact while the body is stabilized and to demonstrate control.

4. Jog and bounce the ball; repeat toss and catch from above.

5. Skip and bounce the ball; repeat toss and catch from above.

Holding the ball high on landing. Demonstrate control.

4'S HIGH-BALL CONTROL

4's high-ball control.

Two or more goalkeepers begin on each end as shown. One line tosses and the other receives. After the save is made, the goalkeeper throws the ball to the next player in the serving line and the two players change lines. Serves should always allow the goalkeeper to move forward to save. Reinforce the footwork, jumping, calling, catching and landing technical points outlined above.

Progression
1. Vary the type and height of the toss.
2. Vary the angle of the toss (force the goalkeeper to move at an angle to save).
3. The serving goalkeeper follows his toss and challenges the goalkeeper with his body, providing realistic pressure.
4. Add another player in the middle of the area to contest each serve.

6'S HIGH-BALL SERVICE

sports-graphics.com

6's high-ball service.

Another means of training high-ball receiving in the club training setting, this environment adds more traffic and variables to the exercise. Three servers toss balls for the working goalkeepers to catch. After each catch, they return the ball to the server and then push through the center of the triangle, where they must have contact with other goalkeepers before stepping into another goal.

Progression

1. Keepers must cover another ball left in front of each goal after each save (rebound).
2. Add footwork (e.g., ladders) for the keepers to do as they pass through the triangle.
3. The server shoots a second ball (rebound) after the goalkeeper controls the high ball.
4. Keepers can come out through a goal together and challenge for the same ball.
5. Add field players around the triangle. These players can challenge for any ball. Any loose rebounds are live to the cone goal.

CATCHING NEAR THE BAR

Catching the ball high near the bar.

For balls shot on frame where the goalkeeper can get to his line, and for those goalkeepers capable of reaching the bar, they should focus on getting and keeping the toes, hips and shoulders all facing up-field. The next step is timing the jump. Young goalkeepers tend to jump early or not at all, so the practice below is an instrumental and incremental teaching tool for learning timing and patience in dealing with high balls from distance.

Simple high-ball catches at the bar.

Here the coach tosses balls underhand up underneath the bar from seven yards out. The goalkeeper focuses on keeping the toes, hips and shoulders all facing the ball and making a clean save up under the bar. The timing of the jump, the positioning of the hands (work together and catch in front of the head, eyes to ball) and clean handling are all critical to building confidence in this situation. Explain that for young goalkeepers, shots from distance (outside the 18-yard box) can be dealt with in this manner because it is not necessary to maintain a high position to cut the angle because at younger ages, the pace of the shots allow the goalkeeper to make the necessary adjustments to stop the ball from the goal line.

Progression

1. The goalkeeper shuffles back and forth. When the coach prepares to serve, he sets his feet and goes up and makes the save (adds movement and reminds goalkeeper to set himself to save). Crucial here is the effort to keep the toes, hips and shoulders facing forward.
2. The coach varies angles and distances of serve.
3. The coach works from beyond the penalty spot, punting balls up near the bar for the keeper to save.

4. The goalkeeper starts at a cone three yards off the line and must retreat to the line to save.

HIGH TIPPING

An emergency save for goalkeepers caught off their line, or in situations where catching is not possible (e.g., damp weather, high winds, heavy-paced shots), high tipping is often not properly taught and not practiced often enough for goalkeepers to become and remain proficient at this important skill.

sports-graphics.com

High tipping: Isolating the skill.

Three goalkeepers form a group. The three get in a line with two servers on the ends and the working goalkeeper in the middle on his knees perpendicular to the servers. One server tosses a ball underhand to the goalkeeper, who tips the ball on to the other server. It is useful in this exercise to have a coach hold a flag or stick above the back shoulder of the working goalkeeper (two feet above the head) to simulate a crossbar for the goalkeeper to tip over.

Key technical points of emphasis

1. Use the near hand to tip (this will be the up-field hand when the skill is put in practice).

2. Point the bottom of the wrist toward the ball and maintain that posture throughout the save. This helps guarantee that the ball will be lifted over rather than thrown into the goal.

3. The contact point is the fingers, which can then help lift the ball. Note that the arm is bent to the point that the elbow is pointing up-field and the hand, at point of receiving, is near the ear.

4. The ball is lifted and pushed above and across the head, with the eyes tracing the save and the fingers extending to give lift.

The ball is then tossed the other direction for the goalkeeper to tip with the other hand back to the first server.

Progression

The goalkeeper works from a standing position. The idea here is that the technique is being practiced in increasingly realistic settings, from kneeling to standing. This progression can be practiced in the goal to allow the goalkeeper to tip over the bar.

High tipping: Working in the goal.

When the goalkeepers have mastered or warmed up the technical skill of high tipping, the next logical progression is to put the goalkeeper in an environment in the goal where he can add footwork and timing to the saving technique. The goalkeeper begins on his line, then comes out and touches the ball being held by the server beyond the 6-yard box. After the drop-step, the goalkeeper recovers to goal and tips the ball served by the coach over the bar.

Progression

1. Balls are served from different angles by multiple servers.
2. The goalkeeper covers an extra ball in the area after the first save (recovery save if tip hits bar).
3. Server hits balls from 18-25 yards after the goalkeeper steps to his 6-yard line.

High tipping: Footwork cues.

1. On recognizing the need to recover and save, the first step is a drop-step (see above) in which the keeper pulls one foot back toward the goal. This movement closes the shoulders to the ball (and they must remain closed to tip well) and indicates which hand will tip. In other words, if the keeper drop-steps with the left foot, the right hand will be used to tip.

2. Shuffle, concentrating on the ball.

3. A cross-over step is used by some goalkeepers but is not recommended, as it can create complications for setting to tip.

When the goalkeeper has arrived in the position to tip, he presents the trailing hand and tips over the bar as described in the base exercise. Note that if the goalkeeper finds he can catch the ball, he should square his feet, hips and shoulders to the ball and make the catch, to avoid conceding a corner kick.

CHIP SHOT

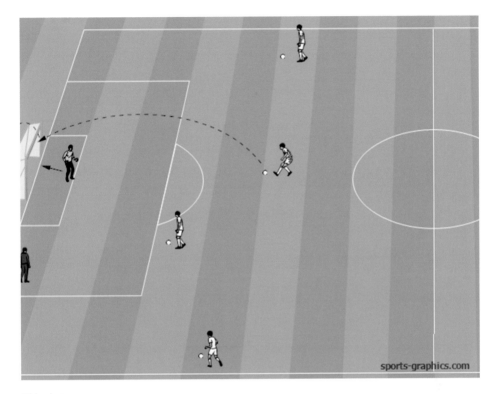

Chip shot.

Shooters spread in an arc with angles ranging between the top corners of the 18-yard box and from varying distances. The goalkeeper stands near the top of his 6-yard box. Shooters try to beat the goalkeeper up under the bar. The goalkeeper must read the shot early, deciding whether to go forward and catch or retreat to catch or tip. Encourage the goalkeeper to catch, rather than tip, as often as possible.

Progression

1. The goalkeeper has footwork (cones or ladder) to do before recovering to the goal to tip. The footwork should be near the top of the 6-yard box, and the attacker only shoots when the goalkeeper gets to the end of the footwork pattern.

2. The goalkeeper starts from a laying position (on his front side) at the top of the 6-yard box.

3. The goalkeeper starts from the top of the 6-yard box, but then takes a set number of steps forward (away from the goal) before recovering to save the shot.

4. Add a recovery save for the goalkeeper from an attacker in the 18-yard box.

CROSSES

Dealing with crosses. The ability to control one's box is critical for goalkeepers aspiring to play at high levels. The topic will be addressed through a variety of exercises, each intended to improve the goalkeeper's range and confidence under pressure.

Starting position for a cross from a wide position.

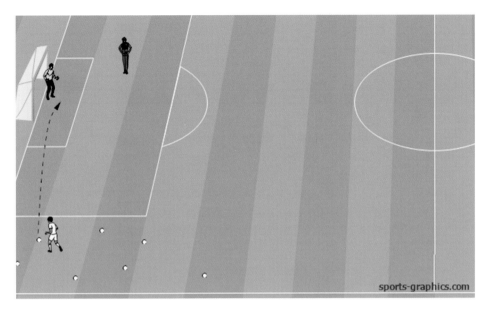

Crosses from wide positions.

A simple but effective means of training the goalkeeper to adopt proper starting positions for crosses from wide areas, this practice pits a coach server against the goalkeeper and can be complicated to challenge senior goalkeepers. The coach can assess the keeper's chosen starting position and his mechanics in dealing with the cross. The variety of serving positions will allow the coach and goalkeeper to discuss starting positions and range for many different crosses.

Variations

1. Work on a specific type or location of cross (e.g., driven balls near post).
2. Add footwork before the cross using cones or ladders.
3. Add finishers who roam the box trying to get on the end of crosses and rebounds.
4. Add defenders. These players must coordinate their efforts with the goalkeeper, who needs to direct them and control the area with increased traffic.

NEAR-POST DANGER

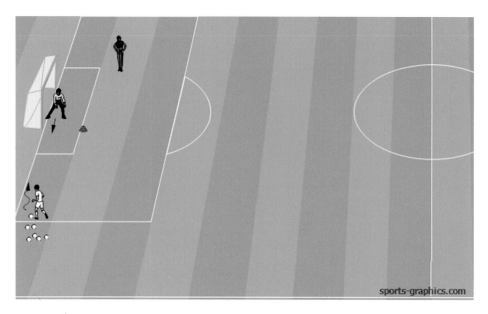

Near-post danger.

Coaching legend Pep Guardiola refers to a driven ball to the near post on a cross as half a goal. The inference is correct that this is a very difficult area to protect, both for the goalkeeper and the defenders. In this exercise, the coach varies his crossing distance along the end line, sometimes striking from just inside the bottom corner of the 18-yard box, sometimes closer and sometimes dribbling toward the goal and then crossing. For the goalkeeper, the general rule is to move toward the ball as it approaches the goal, even getting beyond the post when the ball enters the 6-yard box (because of the danger of a direct shot). Indeed, the goalkeeper must eventually treat the attacker as a breakaway and close down if the run continues to goal. An additional, useful frame of reference for the goalkeeper in this situation is to think in terms of defending two goals. The standard goal is the first concern, but he should also attempt to protect an imaginary goal between the near post and the top of the 6-yard box (delineated with a cone in the diagram and the flag in the photo). This second goal represents a critical danger area, as any ball allowed to pass through will be a tap-in for an attacker. This consideration should make the goalkeeper more aggressive in tight crossing situations.

Variations

1. Add attackers trying to finish in the six-yard box.

2. Add defenders who coordinate defending with the goalkeeper.

Near-post danger.

CROSS AND DISTRIBUTE WITH NUMBER CALLING

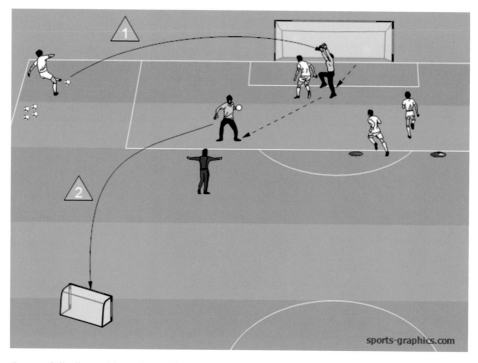

Cross and distribute with number calling.

The server crosses (1). One target harries the goalkeeper as two other targets close into the area. The goalkeeper must holler out the number of fingers held up by the coach after the ball is served. He then deals with the cross and distributes into the goal (2). Calling the number compels the goalkeeper to manage more details and then relocate the ball, complicating the environment.

BACK-POST CROSS AND COVER

Back-post cross and cover.

This environment deals with crosses played into the dangerous back-post area, a notoriously difficult save for goalkeepers. In this case, the keeper fields a series of lofted balls to the back post, focusing on opening up his footwork and hips to pursue the ball and clean appropriate save choices at the back post. After each save, he also gets out and down to cover a ball left at the back corner of the 6-yard box. This last detail adds a second save to the sequence and prepares the goalkeeper to deal with a knock-down or rebound, which are common in this area.

Progression

1. Add attackers who crash the far post and try to finish the crosses.
2. Add defenders who coordinate with the goalkeeper to defend the crosses.
3. Add a shooter at the back corner of the 6-yard box. This player shoots or dribbles to create the second save opportunity.

GOALKEEPER GLADIATOR WARS

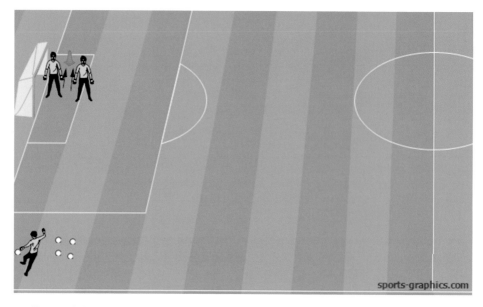

Goalkeeper gladiator wars.

Two goalkeepers defend the same goal. The server hits crosses and the goalkeepers duel for control of the ball. Play until the ball is covered. Vary the serves. Goalkeepers alternate starting positions.

Variations

1. Goalkeepers must touch a cone at the back post then move to take the cross.
2. Add an attacker.
3. Goalkeepers start from the push-up position.

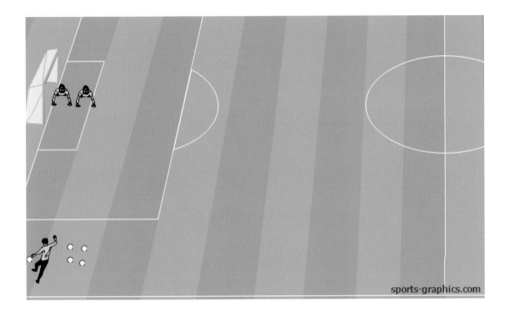

DUELING GOALKEEPERS: CROSSES

Dueling goalkeepers: Crosses.

Here a server crosses balls for two goalkeepers to win. The goalkeepers duel for control of every cross (play until rebounds are covered). A fun variation is to give extra points for punching or boxing the ball into your opponent's goal. Vary the angle, distance and type of service.

Variations

1. Goalkeepers start on their front sides and recover to save.
2. Goalkeepers start on their back sides and recover to save.
3. Add an attacker who may score on either goal.

POWER AND SPEED JUMPING

Power and speed jumping.

A simple, efficient way to work a group of goalkeepers in power and speed jumping. Use a towel, cones or hurdles. The goalkeepers jump side-to-side or over-and-back in patterns set by the coach. Use one or two feet or alternate. Add a shooter on one end who serves a ball to save after a set number of jumps. For speed jumps, see which goalkeeper can complete the most jumps in a 15-second window. Add multiple hurdles to complicate the patterns and increase the workload.

Additional variations

1. After landing on one side, the goalkeeper drops to his front side, recovers and continues.

2. After a set number of jumps, the goalkeeper does footwork around the hurdle and then the sequence continues.

AGILITY LADDER

In and out.

The agility ladder is an outstanding tool for goalkeeper power, footwork and fitness. Use a ball to add a shot and save as the goalkeeper exits the ladder after each sequence to add more functional elements to the training.

Progression
1. Run through the ladder, making one step per rung.
2. Run through the ladder, making two steps per rung (one with each foot).
3. In and out. Start facing across the ladder and step in and out of each run with both feet, one after the other (above).

4. Jump on both feet in each rung, emphasizing quickness.

5. Jump on both feet in each rung, emphasizing height and power.

6. ump on one foot in each rung, emphasizing quickness.

7. Jump on one foot in each rung, emphasizing height and power.

8. Zig-zag. Start with the left foot next to the first rung and right foot in that rung (1); then move both feet in the rung (2); finally, the right foot steps outside to the right and forward of the next rung and the sequence continues.

Variations

1. Add a server who tosses balls for the goalkeeper to catch and return during the footwork sequence.

2. Add a server who shoots a ball for the goalkeeper to save after each round of footwork.

CORE WORK AND CATCHING

Core work and catching.

The goalkeeper lies on his back with his knees bent and feet flat on the ground. When the goalkeeper sits up, his partner pushes a ball for him to catch and return before he repeats the sequence. A medicine ball is an outstanding alternative in this exercise.

Variations

1.   Reverse the order. Toss the ball to the goalkeeper, who does a sit-up and then returns the ball.

2.   The keeper lies on his front side. While the keeper's hands and feet are kept off of the ground, the server tosses balls for him to catch and return.

CONE FLIP

Cone flip.

An exercise that blends competition with targeted fitness for the lower back and hamstrings. Place 30 cones in a 10 × 10 grid, half facing up and half facing down. One goalkeeper tries to get all of the cones facing up, the other to make all cones face down. The players must stay on their feet and can only flip one cone at a time. They may not interfere with the other goalkeeper's efforts. Play for two minutes and then count cones by orientation to determine the winner.

REACTIONS TRAINING PAIRS

This set of reactions training exercises is designed to be mixed in as a warm-up variation, or for a few minutes of intensive training before field players shoot at goal. Note that this is not a stand-alone set (in other words, just mix in one or two of these ideas for a few minutes rather than running through the entire set). In all cases, emphasize stable starting position, concentration on the ball, soft hands, minimizing rebounds and quickly covering any loose ball. In all cases except where noted, perform the exercise for 30 seconds and then switch roles.

1. One goalkeeper holds the ball with hands on the underside of the ball at chest-height while the working goalkeeper holds his hands just above the ball. The player holding the ball drops the ball and the other goalkeeper must catch the ball before it hits the ground. If the goalkeeper is catching every time, encourage the server to fake a release and to hold the ball lower to increase the level of challenge. Which goalkeeper can catch more balls in 30 seconds?

2. Two goalkeepers stand in ready position on opposite sides of a ball on the ground (goalkeepers should be staggered so that they do not knock heads). The coach calls out body parts for the keepers to touch with both hands (e.g., ankles, knees) and then when he calls "Ball!" the goalkeepers try to grab the ball. This is a fun, challenging way to encourage goalkeepers to be quick in getting after a loose ball.

3. Two goalkeepers face one another one yard apart. One bounces a ball off of the other's foot and the goalkeeper must cover as quickly as possible. Alternatively, the ball is live off of the bounce and both goalkeepers seek to cover.

Reactions training with the working goalkeeper starting facing away from the server.

4. The target goalkeeper looks at his feet until the server calls "Shot!" and then looks up to make the save. Emphasize to the server that the ball should be on the goalkeeper's frame and with pace to challenge the goalkeeper.

    •   Standing and serves are from the ground.

    •   Standing and serves are punted.

    •   Target goalkeeper starts facing away and turns to save when the server calls "Shot!"

    •   Target goalkeeper starts on his stomach facing away and then rises and turns to save.

SHOT-STOPPING

Keeper Wars: 1 vs. 1

Keeper wars: 1 vs. 1.

This competitive training environment is recommended as a means of both testing shot-stopping skills and also increasing competitive mentality among the goalkeeping corps. Goalkeepers remain in the goal as long as they score with every shot and also do not allow their opponent to score. If there are only two goalkeepers, keep score in saves rather than goals. Keepers alternate shooting attempts and must shoot from behind the cone line set by the coach. Adjust the goal size and distance to suit the goalkeepers' ages and levels.

Variations

1. Require a certain type of shot to test a training theme or improve a goalkeeper's ability to deal with a particular type of shot. For example, all shots on the ground or chipped (in this case, goalkeepers must start higher and recover to avoid being chipped).

2. No goalkeeper can leave their feet to save. This restriction compels the goalkeepers to move their feet quickly to make saves from a standing position.

3. Any rebound results in the goalkeeper losing a point or being removed if there is a rotation.

DOUBLE KEEPER WARS

sports-graphics.com

Double keeper wars.

Two goalkeepers start in each goal. It is important to stagger the keepers when they are defending (see diagram above) so that there are no injuries. This is a fun, intense variation on the game for a larger group.

•   Attacking goalkeepers can dribble and play 2-vs.-2 to goal. This variation adds a realistic emphasis to the game and compels the defending goalkeepers to communicate and organize their defense.

THE CAULDRON

The cauldron (1).

This is an intensive, flexible environment in which goalkeepers are challenged to deal with multiple tasks. In the base exercise, the goalkeeper does footwork from one post to the center of the goal and then steps forward before diving to save a shot toward the post. He must then recover to cover a second ball (rebound) at the corner of the 6-yard box.

The cauldron (2).

The cauldron (3).

THE PIT

The pit.

Here, the goalkeeper runs or does footwork around any of the balls in the area and then recovers centrally to deal with a shot from the server.

Variation

* Cover any ball in the area after each save.

CONCLUSION

The idea behind this volume was to provide a thorough but accessible explanation of the requirements of the goalkeeping position. In addition, the hope was to share the best of what the authors have learned through decades of playing the position and training professional, college, high school and club goalkeepers. Finally, there has been an effort to think in terms of compiling a big idea book for specialists, team coaches and parents so that the many aspects of playing the goalkeeping position can be trained in varied and challenging environments.

Best wishes in goalkeeper training.

Tony Englund and John Pascarella

APPENDIX A

Goalkeeper Progress Report Form

Date: _____

Coach: _____

Goalkeeper: _____

Basic stance	1	2	3	_____
Footwork	1	2	3	_____
Technical handling	1	2	3	_____
Punching and tipping	1	2	3	_____
Diving	1	2	3	_____
Shot-stopping	1	2	3	_____
1-vs.-1 situations	1	2	3	_____
Distribution	1	2	3	_____
Crosses	1	2	3	_____
Set-pieces	1	2	3	_____
Mental approach	1	2	3	_____

1 = Below standard training target; 2 = Meets standard for level; 3 = Above average for standard; n/a = Not assessed

Overall assessment

_____

Shared with goalkeeper: _____

APPENDIX B

Goalkeeper Match Performance Feedback Form

Date: _____

Coach: _____

Goalkeeper: _____

Positioning	1	2	3	_____
Control of area	1	2	3	_____
Communication	1	2	3	_____
Technical handling	1	2	3	_____
Shot-stopping	1	2	3	_____
Distribution	1	2	3	_____
Crosses	1	2	3	_____
Set-pieces	1	2	3	_____
Mental approach	1	2	3	_____

1= Below standard training target; 2= Meets standard for level; 3= Above average for standard; n/a= Not assessed

Overall assessment

_____
_____

Shared with goalkeeper: _____

SOURCES AND RECOMMENDED READING

Anderson, Chris and David Sally. *The Numbers Game: Why Everything You Know About Soccer is Wrong.* Penguin, 2013.

Bengsbo, Jens. *Fitness Training in Soccer – A Scientific Approach.* Reedswain, 2003

Bischops, Klaus. *Soccer Training for Goalkeepers.* Meyer & Meyer, 2006.

Crust, Lee & Clough, Peter J. "Developing Mental Toughness: From Research to Practice." *Journal of Sport Psychology in Action.*

DiCicco, Tony. *Field session,* 2016 NSCAA Convention.

DiCicco, Tony and Hacker, Colleen. *Catch Them Being Good.* Penguin, 2002

DiCicco, Tony and Hacker, Colleen. *Goalkeeping: The DiCicco Method* (DVD). Soccer Plus.

Englund, Tony. *Goalie Wars! Goalkeeper Training in a Competitive Environment.* World Class Coaching, 2010.

Englund, Tony. *Players' Roles and Responsibilities in the 4-3-3: Attacking.* World Class Coaching, 2011.

Englund, Tony. *Players' Roles and Responsibilities in the 4-3-3: Defending.* World Class Coaching, 2011.

Englund, Tony. *Style and Domination: A Tactical Analysis of FC Barcelona.* World Class Coaching, 2012.

Englund, Tony. *The Art of the Duel: Elite 1 vs. 1 Training.* Foreword by Anson Dorrance. World Class Coaching, 2014.

Englund, Tony. *Competitive Small Group Training: Maximizing Player Development in the*

Small Group Setting. Foreword by Tony Sanneh. World Class Coaching, 2014.

Englund, Tony. *Complete Soccer Coaching Curriculum for 3-18 Year Old Players Volume I.* NSCAA, 2014.

Englund, Tony. *Sporting St. Croix Goalkeeper Curriculum Book.* LuLu, 2015.

Gregg, Lauren. *The Champion Within: Training for Excellence.* JTC Sports, 1999.

Greiber, Peter. *The Complete 'Keeper: Youth Goalkeeper Training A to Z.* Success in Soccer.

Jones, Graham. "What is this thing called mental toughness? An investigation of elite sport performers." *Journal of Applied Sport Psychology.* 2002.

Lyttleton, Ben. *Twelve Yards: The Art and Psychology of the Perfect Penalty Kick.* Penguin, 2014.

Mannix, Patrick. Interview on October 3, 2016.

Manoel, Mateus. Classroom presentation, Sporting Kansas City preseason, February 2015.

McAllister, Josh. Paper on Warm-Ups and Cool-Downs, November 2016.

Mulqueen, Tim. *The Complete Soccer Goalkeeper.* Human Kinetics, 2011.

Pascarella, John. Field session, 2016 NSCAA Convention.

Pascarella, John. Field and Classroom presentations, NSCAA Master Coach Certificate, 2015.

Van Kolfschooten Frank. "How Simple Can It Be? Behind the Scenes with Raymond Verheijen." WFA 2015.

Verheijen, Raymond. *Conditioning for soccer.* Reedswain, 1998.

Welsh, Alex. *The Soccer Goalkeeping Hand book.* Master's Press, 1998.

Wood, Warrick. "Maintaining a Winning Focus is not the Way to Win." *Soccer Journal,* October 2014.

Websites

"The 10 Nutrition Rules to Live By," www.ussoccer.com.

"Nutritional Guide for Soccer Players," www.active.com.

"7 Nutrition Myths for Soccer Players," www.active.com.

CREDITS

Cover design:	Claudia Sakyi
Cover photos:	© picture-alliance.de/dpa
Editing:	Anne Rumery
Typesetting and graphics:	Claudia Sakyi
Interior layout:	Claudia Sakyi
Interior photos:	© picture-alliance.de/dpa:

pp. 14, 35, 46, 49, 50, 53, 56, 58-59, 68-69, 74, 76, 81, 84, 102-104, 106-107, 109-110, 112, 123, 125, 143, 145, 150, 156, 165-166, 169, 171-172, 174, 177, 180, 182, 184, 190, 214, 226, 251-252, 262, 273, 288

© Karen McCullough: p. 75

© Tony Englund: All other photos.